Is God Present In The Quilt

Patrick Raymond

Tellwell Talent
www.tellwell.ca

ISBN
978-1-77302-387-8 (Hardcover)
978-1-77302-386-1 (Paperback)
978-1-77302-510-0 (Ebook)

Table of Contents

The book cover is a photograph of one of the many quilts my mother lovingly put together.

The children in the picture are my granddaughter Sadie and my grandson Jack.

Recent picture at my Brother Roger's 70th birthday

About the author

PERMANENT DEACON PATRICK RAYMOND HAS BEEN married to Denise Ranger for 46 years. He is the father of 3 daughters and grandfather of 5 grandsons and 3 granddaughters. Deacon Pat was born January 02 1948 in Temiskaming Quebec Canada. He is the second son to Jean and Lucille Raymond.

Deacon Pat went to primary school in Quebec and finished high school in Ontario then went to College in Sault Ste Marie Ontario. He worked as a geologist for a mining company for 40 years. In the year 1988, he was accepted to study for the permanent deaconate program. His five years of reparation plus an added year of discernment lead to a recommendation to ordination. He was Ordained to permanent Deacon on May 24 1994 at St. Alexander's parish in Chelmsford Ontario Canada. He is still taking correspondence course towards a degree in Religious Studies at the local University.

Over the years he was involved with the Lions Club and Knights of Columbus. He worked with boys in minor hockey as a coach and executive. He was employed at a local funeral home after retirement.

The unwanted guest in his marriage was Multiple Sclerosis. As the years went Denise found herself handicapped. This has lessened his ability to serve the three parishes he is assigned to. The parishes have been nothing short of prayerful, generous in there kindness and caring. He is home, reaping the fruits of his sacrament of marriage, the grace of caring for his spouse. This has also given him the opportunity to write this book. It was written to give a voice that reminds all of us that even in what seems like idle times, a new life can be found.

I would like to thank my daughter Tyna, my sister Sister Louise and my good friend Elaine Fievoli for their help in editing. Also I would like to thank my daughter Dawn for her artistic gift in the design of the cover. From the very beginning, my daughter Renée has been a strong supporter of this project. All my girls have enriched my life and they continue to be there for dad. My spouse Denise is my critic, my support and my reason for being. Thank you all in this journey to relive these wondrous memories.

Nothing seems real especially reality itself. Too often we find ourselves in what seems real and when we look back nothing is visible. Memories are elusive and are possibly the only reality we have to create the reality we live in. From childhood to present memories, these are the footstools to the future we have to share. Nothing we can dream of or share can be created without strong good or bad memories. Who we are and who people see are a mixture. The sooner we embrace the past , the sooner we can move on to what we can be. Aren't we all a quilt in the making?

Mom Lucille Gagne 18 years old

Jean Raymond 25 years

Wedding picture of Jean Raymond and Lucille Gagne

IS GOD PRESENT
In
The quilt

Preschool Years In
Temiskaming Quebec

MY LIFE IS REALLY NOT THAT INTERESTING BUT THOSE who lived with me, around me or influenced me is truly a miracle. Never in all my wildest dreams did I ever think that being me would ever be of concern to anyone or anything. To discover that in me and around me the presence of someone else is beyond belief. As a child, I had this passion for people from mom and dad. Who would have thought that a Chinese laundry-man would have an impact my life? I can remember from that small home with a porch, I was allowed to reach out in numerous ways either with the Chinese family next door or with anyone else. I would watch with amazement how they would work, clean and iron all those white shirts. I remember the well-dressed people who would come in and complain of too much starch or not enough and then see this gentle man who only wanted to feed his family, bow (as we see in those stereo types on TV) and muttering something in Chinese after the person left and then always look at me with a blank expression. I don't know how much time I spent in what seemed like a hot humid sweat shop but enough to feel the struggle of this man and those (probably his wife and children) who never seem to stop working. I learned that hard work comes from a need to survive. To this day I don't know how this family, who were so far from home looking for a better life. Did they survive or did they die so others may survive? I think in many ways we also make those choices in our lives not as dramatic perhaps never the less we make decisions that change our lives and possibly the lives of those around us. Yes! Even that little boy who is sitting watching you live your life. I thank that gentle man who allowed me to sit and watch his life unfold before me. I would like him to know that even though he may be dead, he continues to live in that little boy from so many years ago.

One thing about that little house was how little room there was. This never stopped us from playing and running around and driving mom crazy. This is the house where Roger brought home mumps and chicken pox. You see, when you lived in such a small house, you look sick and everyone else felt the same. This is the house I swallowed a penny one of those large pennies and mom monitored my poop to see if the penny would get through. I wish it would have been a quarter and pooped two dimes and a nickel. That would have gotten mom's and everyone else's attention. This is also where my older brother and I wrestled and ran around.

Mom was in the background telling us to behave. I was running from Roger in play and I tripped. I went flying (which seemed forever) and hit the corner of the sewing bench. I was scared within an inch of my life and almost took my eye out. There was blood all over. Roger told mom it was an accident. Mom was just happy that we were both okay.

Me on left with Roger. I was 2 and Roger 4

From that same little house in Quebec the local arena was a stone's throw away. I spent a lot of time there one summer when they were revamping the inside. Today this could not have happened, but the man who looked after the place allowed me to pitch my tent of interest without asking; I felt a need to watch this man do what had to be done. He often shared his lunch with me and talked to me like I really existed. Every time I eat a pepperette I am reminded of how he introduced me to them. Oh! How I wanted mom to buy some pepperettes and she said no. So when she went for a nap and I thought I would just borrow some cash and go buy some on my own. The kicker was that I left her purse open. Well, to say the pepperettes were hot, would put it mildly, compared to how hot mom was when I got home. I can still see her face as I arrived home man was mom p---ed. I never knew my mother could be so disappointed and I told her that I just wanted to get some pepperrettes and share them with this man who shared them with me. The punishment was, mom and I went to see my new found friend and I had to explain what I had done and that it wasn't something he had put me up to. After mom left satisfied there wasn't something going on I was allowed to stay and he gently explained to me what I had done was wrong. He was touched that I wanted to return the favor. The other thing I remember was his gentle eyes and his beard. He always took the time to explain to me what he was doing. There weren't many children where we lived and I always found myself elevated to older kids and even adults. That was my comfort zone. I would like to thank that nameless man who cared enough to allow a little boy to feel so important!

There was one sad moment I can remember it was when I started or thought I started school. In grade one I was 5 and going to be 6 Jan 2. The rules stated that I had to be six by Dec 31 and so that made me too young by two days. I was heartbroken and cried all the way home after I had practiced so hard on tying my shoe laces.If I wanted to go to school this was one skill I needed to master. Mom held me so close that day I can still feel her arms around me. I knew things would be okay. Mom was always there to catch me when my world would chew me up and spit me out.

I would also like to thank those older boys who allowed me to play ball with them. You see that house was also across the ball park. When I saw them play ball, I would grab my glove and run to watch and they'd always ask me to play. Man you can't image how special I felt. Once while I was watching the big kids playing I found myself running around with other kids. I was the smart one running with a pocket knife open. Yes, I fell on the knife and it did stick into my stomach. So, I pulled it out, bled a little, and off I went on my way. The big kids took the time to teach me and allow me to make mistakes. They would take turns helping and coaching me even though they didn't have to. I played with my age group in little league but always preferred those pickup games with the big boys. It was the same in street hockey. I was always drawn to the big kids. As I look back, that little house wasn't much to look at but I tell you the view of the outside world was placed before me on a silver platter from the humble beginnings of mom and dad. Thank you!!!!

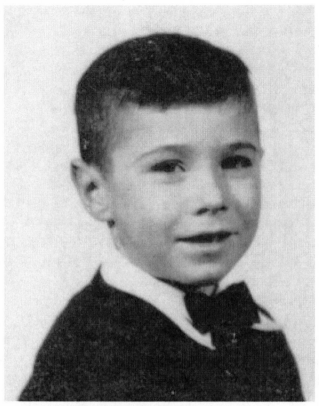

6 years old Grade one 1954

Grammar School Years

SOMETIME LATER, WE MOVED AWAY, ABOUT TWO blocks away into company housing and my life changed. There were other children. Living with peers was difficult because I never felt accepted or important like I did when I was around grownups and older boys. Maybe I was an old soul as they say so I found myself often playing alone. Don't' get me wrong I liked my own company. The Chinese laundry closed, the arena was further away and the ball field was out of sight. All we had was a small back yard full of kids and no room to breathe. I remember one day I was in the field (baseball field).I often went there in hope that I would see the big kids. As I reflect on it now; it's where I could breath. This one day I lay quietly in the tall grass watching the birds flying. As free as birds of course, they would land nearby to eat. So I slowly inched forward to see how close I could get. Well, I got so close that I was able to catch one and I ran home to tell mom. (Yes bird in hand) and all I got was "that's nice now let it go". I never found something so hard to let go. It's almost like I was letting go of all those things that made me special; at the beginning and not in this stinking company house (the house was bigger but it wasn't home). For some reason I felt alone; you know that feeling that even though you're in a crowd you still feel alone? Right behind this little yard was the tennis court. It was reserved for the company executives' families. That's where the big kids played tennis and it was like this awe moment when I spotted some of the big kids I played ball with. It's when they spotted me. My life changed for the better as they invited me to come and play tennis with them. I was in seventh heaven as they gave me an old tennis racket and balls and before you knew it there I was playing tennis. I even got to fill in on a tournament when one player from a pair's team was a no show and I was asked to play. We won! You can't imagine how great I felt. It was probably one of the greatest sport moments in my 10 years.

I learned a lot from those older boys especially in sports. I learned how to have fun. Once when we ran out of tennis balls to play street hockey all we needed was to wait till the milkman made his rounds with horse and wagon and we would have a week supply of pucks as the horse would poop nice round ones for us. They froze in the cold air. We used catalogs for goalie pads and a baseball glove as a catching mitt to help me play goalie. Now we're talking hockey! Maybe that is why I always elevated to them as they didn't have a whole lot of rules to ruin the game. I can remember as a young catcher, in a little league game thinking to myself " I never get to put out anybody". So the next time somebody tried to steal second base I changed that. The first chance I got, I ran out there myself and put him out instead of throwing the ball. Well, you would think that I had just murdered someone or had committed the crime of the century. Everyone yelled at me, especially the parents. That never happened with the big kids. They only stopped the game, talked to me and explained the error and how it should be done and off we went. Not so with all those loud parents and coaches who chastised me to no end.

All was pardoned by the parents (want to be athletes) when we won some little league championship, I remember playing but it meant nothing to me. All I wanted was to play baseball. There was a big banquet and a lot of speeches, all I know is that I walked away with this really neat jacket with neat crest. For the longest time I didn't feel like a champion until I found myself playing with the big kids who made me feel that I had accomplished something? The adults or organizers always made me feel nervous and never good enough. Mom and dad, being new to this world, being from the farm life, had really nothing to say except good boy. That's all I needed to know. They saw me as a good boy.

The same thing happened when we won the peewee tournament for the first time in North Bay. Everyone was cheering and made such a fuss over what I thought was just a hockey game that we won. It's almost like they had won some great event, fulfilled a dream that they had for so many years. Never had this small town in Quebec near North Bay ever defeated them in their own back yard. We conquered, they feasted, life went on as always; I wasn't any different, just a little boy who enjoyed playing a game that I continued to enjoy till I was 40. I would like to thank those older boys who gifted me with such a passion for baseball, hockey and all sports, that adults tried to rob me, with expectations, demands, rules and their dreams.

Our next door neighbor, Mr. Roy became my new best friend. He took me under his wing. I spent many days with him in his garage where he built cedar canoes. I can remember the smell of the cedar and how he would take every piece of wood (ribs) and bent it so it would conform into the shape of the canoe. We talked and he explained and answered every question I put to him. Again I felt important and real. For it happens so often in families that moms and dads are so busy with life that they don't always find time to sit and talk and answer your questions. Sometimes you feel that you don't exist for you get no responds to your WHY. Mr. Roy was probably the one person, I missed the most when we moved away. I can still see him working away on those canoes. He always took the time to look at me and smile (God that felt good). May God bless you Mr. Roy. I will always remember you calling your new dog Pat. You can't imagine how proud I was that you cared enough to use my name to be part of your family.

Me with Mr. Roy's dog Pat

Pete the shoemaker was another character that I had the pleasure of meeting who had a huge impact on me. It was all because I was sent to get my new shoes fitted with clickers, you know the metal they put at the toe and heal of the shoe to make them last longer. As I sat there waiting for Pete (an old refugee from Poland or Germany I don't know but his English was bad on a good day) to put on these clickers. In walked Father Clatt with a pair of shoes that seemed okay to me. They became the instruments in me witnessing evangelization before it became the new way of being catholic

That is when I first witnessed this really great priest talking to Pete about faith and church and about what they had talked about before (from what I heard this seemed to be an ongoing thing). I could tell that Pete had issues about faith. I can still hear Father Clatt being ever so gentle and concerned with Pete's questions and doubts. That day my shoes got what was needed for a longer life, but I got more out of it than both men could ever imagine. I got a life infusion of faith in my parish priest. I wish I would have told him this. Who knows, it might have been good for him to know that in trying to convert an old man, he affirmed a young boy's faith. God does work in mysterious ways. God is always gentle and in secret without realizing it. God has instilled in me the compassionate and understanding God.

I made few friends in that neighborhood and one was a kid mom and dad (mostly mom) didn`t want me to play with.I don't know if it was because he was a bad kid or maybe that his dad was a drunk. But I have one good memory and that is when his dad would make home-made root beer. He would put it in actual beer bottles and we would be walking around with beer bottles in our hands. Of course we drove mom and other parents crazy and of course anytime you could do something seemingly wrong in front of parents and didn't do wrong you had to embrace. The other friend was Mitchell, a native kid, in fact his grandfather was an Iroquois chief, so we were told, and he always had all kinds of toy guns. We would meet at his place and he would hand out his guns and holster for us and we would play cowboys and Indians on the one specification that he was always a cowboy. It didn't matter all I cared was that I got a gun to play cowboys and Indians.

The one memory that I remember with great fondness was the times we went swimming at the river or lake. We would leave in the morning with a lunch and go swimming in an area with board walks all around these huge rocks. We would pick a spot and stay all day swimming but most of all because the lifeguards would practice lifesaving techniques with live volunteers. We waited till the girl lifeguards would be up and volunteer to be the drown victims and they would perform mouth to mouth resuscitation. It was our way of getting a taste of the forbidden fruit – every now and then they would throw in a guy and then we would draw straws to see who would be the sacrificial lamb so that the rest of us would get a chance to make our day.

There was that one time I had entered my name in a draw at the grocery store.In those days' moms and dads sent their children to get bread and even cigarettes. The draw was for a bicycle that I really wanted. I must have put in 100 entries. Anyway I didn't get the bike but second price was waiting for me one day as I got home. It was a Bick's Pickle transport (truck and trailer) sitting on the floor of the living room.It was cool but mom only allowed me to play with it indoors .My second daughter has that very truck to this day. (I promised the first grandson would get the truck). Its funny how out of a wish for one thing and receiving another would be a sign of handing down ones history to another's future? If I would of won that bike I wouldn't have had this to share.

Truck I won in draw

Maybe the two men who had the most impact on me were my dad and my grandfather. My grandfather (pepere Raymond) the poster child for all grandfathers with a nice round belly and a balding head with a laugh that could melt the coldest heart and who had the disposition of a teddy bear. Next to my dad the most gentle man I have yet to meet. Granddad worked for the town and I remember him being the garbage man with horse and wagon. He always took the time to slow down so we could hop on for a ride

What a thrill for a four year old that saw no danger and trusted in this gentle man. From that wagon is where my first school bag (leather attaché case thrown out by the big shots) came from. A leather strap was missing so dad brought it to Pete. He sewed on a new strap and off I went, even to high school with this new found treasure, one man's junk is another man's treasure as they say. Later on as I was going to school I often saw pepere as he was now on the road crew and he always made it a point by telling the other men" that's my grandson". I almost grew a few more inches and I walked straighter responding "bonjour pepere".

My dad was a bigger version of my grandfather but with the same joy for life "joy de vive" and gentleness. I wish I would have gotten closer to dad but dad was a man's man, tools, cars, firewood, demolition and construction all areas that were less suited for my skills. You know it was like no matter how many times I cut the piece of wood it was always too short. Yes I was a mommy's boy and proud of it. You got a problem with that, talk to my mom. This really came to light when dad started building a new house in the foreign land of Bonfield, Ontario. During the summers of 1958-59 and 60 he would take my older brother Roger and me along to help him. In fact he had my brother and I gather nails around a school that was being built where my old ball field was. We would then bring these crooked nails home to our dismay to straighten and save on nails. Well dad soon found out that having Roger, my brother, was a lot of help for him and that I on the other hand needed help when it came to hammering and sawing.

In fact, I think that's why my fingers are so short today. Because of this experience I have a fear of hammers and saws (there must be a name for this disease like toolafobia). He would always start the day thinking he had found the perfect job for me but only to his dismay ended up saying: "just go help your mother".

The treasure or gift he left was more spiritual than physical and he probably never knew it. As a teenager, I saw him after a hard day's work and kneel by his bed and pray. There were also times , when he would get up early (real early) so that he could attend mass on Sunday before going to work (there was no Saturday mass). These are the gifts my dad left me. I thank God for this man who could be frustrated by a boy, who preferred to dream than to change the oil in the car, or would rather go swimming than to hammer a nail or even watch him work rather than working. I wish I could have been closer to him.I knew he loved me as we wrestle in the living room. It was his way to touch his boys in a world where men didn't hug men or boys. He had great respect for mom as he would make sure anytime there was manual work such as washing the floor he had his boys do it for her. He told mom that he was proud of me and my brother and that he loved us.I have but one wish or regret and that is I wish he would have told me himself. Love you dad. All these men in my life tells me that God was always present.

back Row: Left to right Sister Louise,
Claudette and Rose-Marie
front :Row Me, Mom (Lucille) and Roger

I have but one brother older than me and not as cute as me and that would be Roger. We shared a lot of life together as we are only 1.5 years apart. The one memory I have of Roger is the day on the bridge when he suggested that I stick my head though this guard rail with circles between bars. So I stuck my head through the circle portion and yes, couldn`t get my head out. Only with the help of fireman and an anxious mom was I able to keep my head on my shoulders. There was also the time we were waiting at the church for altar boy practice. As we waited friends and possibly Roger suggested I should stick my tongue on the metal guard rail (winter) and yes I took the dare. The rest is history as the sisters tried to release me I left a part of my tongue on that railing. I fondly remember those Saturday mornings as we waited to go to play hockey. We would turn the living room into a war zone. Using the elastics mom had made to hold the shin pads (hockey) as ammo. They were perfect. They were just the right size and man they were accurate. You couldn't ask for better ammo at 7 am on Saturdays. The war ended when the peace core (mom) came downstairs threatening us with jail time and torture if we didn't clean up and cease fire. Then she added "there better not be any elastics missing" or hell would be are only destination. This wasn't our first rodeo as we always kept some previously used elastic in storage for just these occasions. (I guess that would be our war chest).

Roger was the seeker of attention as for example he once hit or crushed his index finger and you would think it was the end of the world and a little blood and a rush to the hospital. When he had his tonsils removed later on, I think it was all a cry for attention.

I can always remember those summer nights, when we were allowed to stay up a little later we spent them looking out of our bedroom window across the tennis court at the main fairway (road). We would pick one side or the other and would watch to see who would have the most cars come from that direction (2 points for trucks) something like that. We often got into small arguments but by in large these were good moments topped by mom bringing up sliced oranges sprinkled with salt as a treat (yes oranges were a treat). This was always mom's way of saying "time for bed". After you finished those oranges, time for bed so we would take forever or at least till were heard (vous ete pas coucher encore) (are you two still up). There were less friendly moments as when mom insisted that Roger take me along with his friend Beaver. This was never a request as such, so reluctantly he agreed. It was just my luck that every time this happened, Roger and his friend were planning on playing wrestling and since there was only three of us it would be them against me.

I guess they thought I would get scared and leave (their form of guerrilla warfare) but there was no way I was going anywhere. No matter how much pain I felt or how much humiliation that I had to endure, I wasn't going anywhere. "Bring it on!" I would tell myself. What could go wrong? I was with my big brother and nothing else mattered. These moments were less frequent unfortunately as we had our own friends and I tended, by choice, to fly solo. I sought out adventure (dreams) over pals and buddies. As I reflect on those days I now see the reason. I sought out adults and older kids. They could give me what I couldn't find in my peers and that was a sense of adventure unimaginable. I was often the kid looking "in" rather than the kid looking out. Yet never lonely. I guess mom understood me better than most and she was always a sheltered cove in times of doubt, stormy weather and broken dreams. I love my brother. He means the world to me. I hope he is blessed with a brother as much as I am to him.

There were only three of us in the Quebec adventure called family. The third member is my sister Louise. She has always been a joy and a pain to me in early life but I love her dearly. I often felt I was there to watch over her, to be her homeland security. One time we were being babysat by this teenager (witch) who was having problems of her own and found her to be unusually mean to Louise. I challenged her methods and she became even more abusive. So as small as I was (8 or 9) I took her on and kicked her out of the house. Nobody was going to lay a hand on my sister except me. If I did get it on with my sister my brother Roger always saw fit to put me in my place but always did Roger and I watch out for her.

The year was 1956 when the movie Ten Commandments came to town. A must see movie by all good Catholics. Well, I couldn't wait so I chose to see the movie in French as the first showing was in French. The next day I had a dime left so I asked mom if I could go to the comic book store and buy a comic (yes only a dime). The one thing I hadn't plan on was that the comic book store was part of the theater complex. The other thing I didn't plan on was that I could go if I took Louise with me. Well as we got there we went by the entrance of the movie house and nobody was there, , no usher, no ticket taker, nobody, so I asked Louise if she would like to see the movie and she said yes. So being a good brother, we sneaked in and found two seats. Yes, the nun and the deacon sneaked in without paying to see the Ten Commandments I guess God is a forgiving God. After the movie, we bought our comics and sat down the counter for a pop. Louise and I had fortunately had our allowance. (My sister Louise would like to mention she only got 0.25 and the boys got 0.50 and is claiming (sex discrimination). I would like to remind her that I just took her to the movies. Well Roger was there and he saw us and well you can imagine what hell feels like after Roger leaked it to mom. We were sent to the corner for time out as Roger read our comic books.

There is that one time when I just got my driver's license and Louise needed a ride to go somewhere and dad said I could take her. But unfortunately I had a slight misjudgment with the car and I made her promise not to tell dad and she said she wouldn't. Well, the minute she got half way through the door she told dad everything. She also refused to go to bed when I came home from college and Denise was over, and she was ready to watch the sun rise to make sure that Denise and I didn't have some time alone. I wonder if she was a secret agent sent by mom. Louise insists she was just a chaperon. She grew up and was a solid pillar for mom after dad passed away helping mom with the two younger girls at home. She taught for 32 years and after mom passed away she felt the call to religious life. She followed her dream of becoming a sister of the Precious Blood. As I reflect in some ways she gave up her dream so that others might hope to dream. God was present. We just didn't see it. I think I did pretty well as now she is a nun of the Precious Blood order. Really mom and dad you did well.

Altar server 7 years old

Finally one small story before we move to Ontario. As a small boy, I was always drawn to the church, I was an altar boy. Sunday mass is where I found peace and felt at home.

Two things continue to follow me even today. First it was those small brown envelops handed out by the sisters to instill in us a willingness to give to the church. (maybe it was a fund raiser I don't know) pennies to nickels and dimes whatever (the kicker) we were thought that this would be a true expression of our commitment to the Church. By saving a portion of your allowance (which was like manna from heaven) would be a wonderful way of being Church. We got an allowance when mom had left over money and that was as scarce as a five legged horse. It did happened that we got a quarter every now and again and with that you could buy a pop (Coke tall bottle), chip (Hostess) and a chocolate bar (Sweet Marie). So the trick was when these miraculous days came, you ran to the corner store before the guilt got his ugly hands on our quarter. If you were fast enough, you got your treats, felt sorry that you forgot, shrugged your shoulder and enjoyed every sweet - salty bit.

Secondly it would be that there was always confession once a month on Saturday mornings for us bad kids. It was also, as I now reflect, one way of getting us out of the house and out of mom's hair. Anyway it was an opportunity to shed the guilt of those chocolate bars and chip washed down with the sweet nectar of a coke. This one particular Saturday Roger and I went and after I had spilled my guts out to the priest and got my penance. I retreated to my favorite corner. There I began my chat with God, the Father, (it's funny I can never remember seeing Jesus as separate from God to me it was always God period). Anyway, there I was literary physically; talking and being very much into it, so much so, those others kids started laughing at me. I never heard them until Roger shook me into reality and told me to stop people were laughing at me. I remember this as it was probably the last time I truly felt that close to God. That day was the last day I think I really prayed or really talked to God. I know God was present then and because of that day I know God is present today. I pray that one day I can go back to that little boy and tell him "this is good. Hold on to it as it's a gift" (present from God).

Now school in those days was for me something I looked forward to as my older brother was already going and I wanted to be like him. I did well coming in second or third in those early years. But there was always that one kid who shined beyond recognition and it was always the best of the best. His name was Pierre (the son of a big shot at the mill).

The years went by quickly in grammar school until the year my first communion was jammed pack with memories that had little to do with communion it was more to do with the short pants that came with the suit that mom thought I looked so cute in (never mind that it was really cold that day as we walk to church). I think dad was working (shift work at the paper mill) but it was all worthwhile as after the sisters raved about how all the boys with shirt pants were so well behaved (I guess it took us that long just to thaw out). Mom was so proud and that was enough to melt away any ill feelings. My confirmation changed everything especially after talking to the bishop. He asked me the name of my teacher and I for the life of me couldn't remember her name but I knew she drove a Volkswagen beetle and so I told the bishop that she was the teacher who drove a Volkswagen beetle (rare at the time). Again I found myself in hot water as this teacher heard about it and confronted me with outrage and anger of disproportionate measure that I didn`t know her name. You would have thought I had just shot her dog or cat. I wonder if she's still driving that car. Point of interest for those preparing the students for the sacrament be clear and interesting for if not they may be like, me, who remembers only two things from that time. One was that we filled the church with candidates and secondly that I promised not to drink till I was 21. I broke that promise and I am really surprised that I am still catholic. So teachers of the sacraments please remember it's for and about the kids not mom and dad. Make the sacrament the main focus. The kneeling, walking and bowing are good but they are not the sacrament.

Just a thought that maybe the coolest birthday gift (having a birthday so close to Christmas is not cool) I got was a shinny large flashlight. I didn't think it was that cool till all the guys couldn't get over how lucky I was. Anybody got batteries!!!

The Teens Oh! What Horror!!!!!!

Grade 12 Graduation

THE SUMMER OF 1960 WAS MY "D" DAY. WE MOVED TO the foreign land of Bonfield Ontario (2 hours away). It might as well have been Russia. I really didn't want to move. I was months away from the age of 13 (I didn't know what that meant then) but my body was changing and now this. I was going to small farm town, more cattle than people, an outdoor rink, NO ARENA, relatives coming out of the woodwork and cousins big and small. The one thing that really cramped my style was that there was a lot of eyes watching my every move (one aunt in particular know as the broadcaster). It didn't matter what I did, mom knew about it even before the evil deed was done (blame mom for this with her bragging about me etc.) Anything I did bad back home in Quebec was always with kids my own age (always chose the wrong friends mind you). We smoke cigarettes or (use your imagination) anyway we could get away with most of the stuff. I really didn't feel that people applauded my arrival and probably the one thing and possibly the only thing (this is how I felt) that was happy to see me were the black flies (French cuisine from Quebec) and man they were hungry. Later on I remember my youngest sister, Claudette, who loved playing outside with these blood dripping thick ears as the black flies would just feast on her as she seem immune to the itch.

Anyway we settled in a 66% finished home as money was tight and dad would finish it whenever he could. He had to travel back and forth. He still worked at the paper mill in Quebec (happy wife happy life) and mom was happy as mom was home. The house was on a property that her father gave them. My precious grandmamma Gagne lived behind us, separated by a baseball field, and our humongous garden (all part of the previous farm) that dad saw as the answer to all our prayers. And so began my hatred of gardening as Roger and I had the envious task of weeding and hoeing this garden that went on forever and a day. A note here, is that dad's answers to a rich crop was cow manure and trust me there was a lot of manure around. He was right. Everything grew bigger and stronger including the weeds I digress.

You heard me mention about a baseball field. For a minute I thought I was back at that little house and all those great memories. So as soon as we moved in I looked through every box I could until I found my baseball glove and of course, I took off and never heard those come back here (viens ici). I was sure if I got to the ball field those older boys would magically appear.

I did manage to join a baseball team not the caliber of back home. It was more pick up ball with cousins and their friends. When the men's team came out to practice I was out there like a dirty shirt, I would run after any ball that got by them; picked up the bats and brought them water, anything to be part of my pass.

Roger made the men's team. It was a small town, few players, and Roger was a good ball player, and he could hit. Eventually, they let me practice with them and no matter what they threw at me or how much it hurt they would never see it in my face. I could catch and run with the best of them but hitting was the dent in my armor and kept me off the team until one day they needed a right fielder (not my position) but who cares. I would get to play with the big boys again and I thought I have arrived. It almost felt like home and that little house became more and more a distant memory. It faded away enough that I could move on. So every time I found myself free I was out there in the field helping clean and cutting the grass. If some older boy was practicing I would catch for them, run after the balls that got away, anything to keep my finger on the pulse of what seemed like the only thing to do in this foreign land.

I got to know my cousins more and more as we played ball together. I found out that their interest was more on hunting and playing in the forest behind my grandma's house. As we got to know each other we banded together and formed these cowboy and Indian games and war battles that consumed more of my time. We built forts, camps anything we wanted. There was a freedom I never experienced before. We hunted birds and rabbits, caught frogs and went fishing. On hot days, skinny dipping as the fish weren't biting. This is where Huckleberry Finn came to life for me in so many ways. This is the life I was now experiencing and enjoying. Yes, we even built a raft. We built this hut in the backwoods and got some backseats of cars from my Uncle Leo's garage. We must of dragged, carried them for a mile or so. These seats became beds for a sleepover and seats as we read comic books on those lazy days. The summer experience of those few earlier years were some of and possibly the only teen years I remember and smile at. In the fall we ventured into hunting partridge and rabbits, I never really like this part. In the winter I would come home from school and as soon as I could I would take off with my cousins and go skiing until dark. We would go into the woods where there was what seemed like a large valley and we would go up and down as many times as we could. Oh how I loved those skis!

The rude awakening happened when school started and I found myself in a heap of trouble. As I was the new kid on the block and this new kid refused to pay homage to the local hoods and bullies. My older brother told me to back off and life would be easier. What did he know? He was only my big (more like older he was always smaller than me) brother and I knew better. I refused to be bullied. As I never experienced this before, I wasn't about to start - fights at recess – fight my way home every night as the same snooty kid tried to impress his older brothers by challenging me. I put him down every time, never hitting him. But then his older and bigger brother would come to his rescue and slap me around until I could get loose and run home (good practice for my future career in running track).

These challenges even spilled over into the sacristy at church. As I was getting ready to serve mass (4 pm mass during the school year) and he came in and dragged me outside only to have the same result. The older brother never got his licks in, as Father Rochfort came to my rescue. God love him, he was the next man to come into my life and bless me with challenges and wisdom.

It got so bad that I dare not go out at night. They only lived down the road. Then all of a sudden the harassment stopped. Maybe it was because the older boys were off to another school (reform). Even with this behind me, I still missed home (Temiskaming) and my childhood. Winter came and so did hockey. Mind you, it was played on an outdoor rink but hockey never the less.

I wanted to try out with the older boys like my brother but dad had promised my uncle Ben, the coach of the team of my age group, that I would play goal for him as he truly needed a good goalie (first Bonfield player to be drafted or traded).

I did not enjoy organized hockey that year (for the first time). But there was always pick up hockey and that's when I was almost back home playing with the older kids (note to those who think this as charming and sweet). I want you to know that every time I played on that outdoor rink I would freeze my feet, go home, cry as they thawed out, and get ready for tomorrow's game.

The following year I made the older team and then the men's team (small town if you could skate you made the team lol). This is about the same time things started to change. For example, we (14-15) would go early in the morning to clean off the snow so that we could play shinny hockey before the older (16-19) boys would rise from their midday sleep and ceremoniously kick us off the rink. They could play even though we got the ice ready for us to play. No matter! This is when I realized I wasn't home anymore. I wasn't that little boy that the big kids invited into their sacred space. I wasn't that cute little boy who would look up to them. I was now a threat, a final view of their fading youth and a reminder to them that they were becoming adults (physically anyway).They too, in some way, like me couldn't go back home. They were getting closer to a time that "I didn't know or oops" had no more magical power to forgive them their errors and mistakes. Now they would need to answer for not only the good they did but also the not so good parts of their lives.

Among all of this big bang theory in my life there came an angel, a woman and a new bright light in a young man's life that continuous to touch me even today over 50 years later.. This breath of fresh air was my grandmamma Gagne, my mom's mother who lived in an old farm house behind us just past the ball field. She was short like mom and they looked a lot alike. We were often called to come over and chase the cows out of her garden or shoot the groundhog who insisted on using her garden as a salad bar. We would run over there and she would have the 4-10 ready and loaded. Oh man was that ever a hoot! (Never did hit that groundhog; I think it was intentional as if we did we wouldn't get to shoot that gun again; only wish Roger would of let me shoot). It's when I hit the age of 16 that I truly got the gift of a truly wonderful person that possibly changed my life. Every Friday night after school my cousin, a year younger, (both her Godsons) we would go for supper at her house and we would talk about everything and anything but mostly about scripture. She would read a passage and she would try to explain it to us until it was time for bed (you talk about evangelization). This went on for about a year. Then she got cancer and went away for treatment. I guess they didn't keep me informed. I kept asking about her and I was pushed aside. All these so call cousins who were never around came out of the woodwork. Then grandmamma came home. She looked old (grey hair that she didn't have before), frail, not the grandmother I knew. And then entered the well to do so call adults I really never got to say goodbye (they never acknowledged the little boy sitting in the Chinese laundry). I did serve at her funeral, got to shed a tear. The feeling that I was left with is one of great loss and a disdain for adults as they seem to me to be like vultures surrounding a person that was so much more than they could even imagine. Love you grandmamma. I miss you. Thank you for seeing that little boy in me.

Probably the one person that always saw me as that little boy was mom as much as I grew up and had a family of my own, job etc. I was always her little boy. Mind you I kind of liked being a mommy's boy. She knew how I felt or knew that something wasn't right and always tried to help me through it. She could never do enough. I can recall, mom successfully grew a tulip in a pot in the middle of the winter and she was so proud of it. Only now I have even come close to understanding how much growing this tulip meant to her. We are talking about a women who could do great things the only thing that held her back was the times she lived in. This tulip was her way of saying 'I AM HERE HEAR ME ROAR" . Yet she willingly gave it to me simply because I asked. She had a green thumb that would have put the Green Giant to shame. Mom won countless awards at the fair every fall for her flowers (Louise and I entered the same fair with a bouquet of our own of what we thought were wild flowers but as it turned out there was a mixture of domestic and wild flowers so we were automatically disqualified).

Any way, I had a crush on this grade 4 teacher and I asked mom if I could have the tulip for my teacher. She gave it to me, and the teacher was pleased and amazed that my mom could grow a tulip in the middle of winter. Here I was, so proud of mom and so in love with my teacher, the world was a good place to be in.

When mom took me aside in a very dark time as I was about 17 or 18 and really struggling with relationships, friendships, measuring up and never fitting in where things seemed normal (always was a loner but for some reason that no longer was the right pair of shoes for me; life changed and I didn't or didn't want to. Yet I knew I had to. You see the confusion). Mom picked up on it and she sat me down and talked to me. (I knew she had more on her plate) I don't know how long we talked but I felt better after and knew I had a safe haven in mom if the need arose.

My last year of high school were dark days as far as the relationship with mom and that closeness soured as we fought almost every day over what seemed important to me. As I look back probably what it was is a breaking away from the apron strings difficult as it was for both of us. She could no longer be the harbor for my damage ship as I ventured into a sea of unknown pain and jubilation, of awareness and confusion, of love and broken hearts. I would captain my own ship hoping I was ready. I did come back to that safe cove one day long after as I was visiting her with my spouse and three girls and expressed I was tired. Without a moment's hesitation she told me to go lay down on her bed. I agreed and in she came and tucked me in like I was 5 or 6 again. I knew then that even though I thought I was out to sea on my own that the mother ship was never far away. I remember. The girls teasing me about me being a mommy's boy and I proudly agreed. Mom taught me to pray, the need for church, to be polite and respectful, to be generous, firm yet fair. I saw mom struggle a lot in my teen years as money was tight. She was a proud women and I think sometimes she was frustrated by the fact that her hands were tied under the circumstances that were out of her control (now that's probably where I get it from). She read and quilted, made meals out of nothing and always ate last making sure we were fed. Her escape was her garden (flowers) and pride in her children . We all made life hard for her at times. On the last days off her life we were all with her. For ten days we shared in being there for her; as she laid dying, God was present. She died peacefully and quietly with Louise as her side. I was able to celebrate at the funeral mass as deacon. She always wanted me to be a priest, but she settled for a daughter in law, three grandchildren, 8 great grandchildren and a deacon. I was able to do the homily and make mom proud. I do miss the first women that I loved and hope that I can do the same for my children.

Mom and dad were good parents, a combination of weakness and strength, love and very little hate, love and more love, visionaries for their children, nearsighted for their own future. They had dreams!!!!!! The flaws they had were as important to all of us children as were there strengths. Dad's sense of working 18 hours a day to provide for his family and of mom working cleaning houses so we could have our own home one day was not wasted on us. I miss wrestling with dad, playing cards with him even though he liked to cheat, to see him dance and play the fiddle are memories that are etched in my mind and soul. How mom was able to create art out of a blanket (quilt), oil paintings and most of all the wondrous meals she was so proud of making as the years got better. She gave us a picture book of recipes (our favorites recipes) as a the X-Mass gift before she died. Maybe she knew this was going to be the last X-Mass with us. May God welcome you home and bless you both with rest and eternal happiness as we know God is present.

Back To School

OUTSIDE OF THE FIGHTING EVEN THE REST OF THE scholastic year wasn't much better. Even English as far as social was better than most being from an English neighborhood, but scholastically I was one step from a total wreck. My grammar and spelling were in the toilet and to this day I still find myself using the plunger in the written word. Grades 8 and 9 were at best a report card were hellish as my English marks were reddish. Even though I skipped a grade moving from Quebec to Ontario, within 2 years I adjusted it by flunking grade 9.

Yet I still managed to find shelter in my second home where grades never mattered and that was the local Church. Father Rochfort was the pastor and wouldn't you know it, I was the one who served at his first mass after ordination in Temiskaming (same diocese). This early tie and my frequent presence helped form a

connection much like a student and mentor relationship (he was the brother of my uncle Ben). I was willing
and eager to serve Mass even at the 7:00 am masses
even during the summer (especially in the summer).
With a few other boys (cousins) we went fishing almost
every day and Father had some hot spots. It was too
far for us to bike or walk. We would catch speckle trout
in the 100's and that made mom happy as she could
never get enough speckle trout especially when she was
pregnant for my second youngest sister (Rose) (Pepsi
was the word of the day when Claudette came along 5
years after). The other times we went fishing was with
Marquis and Robert (my cousins). Sometimes we walk
for miles. This reminded me of Huckleberry Finn's life
style from fishing, hunting, building forts or cabins in
the woods.

I worked with Father Rochefort and helped to form
a youth group. He allowed us to use the parish hall on
Friday nights for dances. We had to find an adult to
supervise and Mrs. Sampson was more than willing to
help and off we went. We were a success as there was
nothing else to do in this country town. We bought a
sound system, records and even gave my older brother's
band their first gig. I was the treasurer and DJ. Then I
had my financial windfall when they were looking for
someone to look after the church and hall and I said
I would do it for five bucks a week. This meant I had
to leave my career with Cecutti's bakery where I sold
bread on Saturdays door to door for over 2 years (it paid
$2.00 a day (5am to 7pm). This gave me a raise of 150%.
However it did mean I would have to clean, wash and

wax the church and parish hall floors every Saturday and shovel the walk and stairs on Sunday morning if it snowed the night before. This meant I could buy my own hockey sticks and smokes. I was rich and debt free. Father really got to know me as we often talked. So when these priestly orders came around looking for candidates for junior seminary, Pere Rochefort approached me, without hesitation. He knew this was not for me and steered me away from making a huge mistake.

During this time of change after change and almost 10 years after my sister Louise, the birth of Rose Marie, the stork decided to make an appearance much to my mother's surprise (according to mom this was all my father's doing and I thought you think?) and wouldn't you know it, the stork made another appearance with my now youngest sister Claudette(I didn't dare ask if this had to be dad's fault again). LoL. Claudette the baby was all but 4 when I got married and in a lot of ways I was more like an uncle to her than a brother (3 years at college). Yet I remember I changed her diapers as well as Rose's as I often got up before anyone else and so mom could sleep in. I would change them and feed them and then go to church (as I write this no wonder I couldn't get a date).That plus these were not so good years as far as looks and as well being tongue tied. Remember once taking Rose for a carriage ride and in my adolescent brain storm I thought she would like more speed so I started running and quickly discovered that carriage wheels don't do well in gravel roads. You guessed it! We crashed! Fortunately, except for a little dirt, she was fine. It was especially good that mom never found out. This should have been my first clue, red flag that in my teen year's girls would be the cause of so many less than positive experiences for me. I got into fights (because of a girl), I took unreasonable risks, picked up by the police, had my heart broken and suffered the inability to think straight or speak.

Fights and a loss of common sense! Well, I was dating this one girl (her name is never to be mentioned in this house or anywhere near my spouse) (another story). In Bonfield on Saturday night there wasn't much to do except skating at the outdoor ring and hold hands. I digress. This one Saturday we were to meet at the rink and getting there early I brought my hockey stick and practiced till she made her grand entrance. I ceremoniously planted my stick in the snow bank. Well wouldn't you know it along came the town bully (another meathead with arms the size of tree trunks and the brain of a hockey puck) who was wearing boots. He grabbed my stick and started to play with it (important to remember he was not on skates and important fact for later) (also this stick I bought with my $2.00 a day job - a $1000.00 stick by today's standard) and so I asked him to put the stick back. He said no so I told him it wasn't a choice (you have to understand my girl friend was right there). He just smiled and kept playing with my stick performing for his entourage of idiots (yes even now it upsets me). The smart thing to do was to walk away and hope he would get bored and leave, but no, I had to grab what was mine (remember he had at least 40lbs or more on me) and he threw a punch and I ducked being on skates I was faster and eventually I was able to get him in a headlock. For the life of me I was not going to let go. He wiggled and punched. But not even Hercules could have freed him. That's how strong fear is. Fortunately someone had the common sense to get the parish priest who came and broke it up. This brush with death wasn't all bad as I was now known as the only guy in town to take on this bully and lived to tell about it. Nobody ever challenged me after that. I wonder do girls or women know the power they possess. lol.

Getting picked up by the police was because of this unmentioned girl and the reason for me getting picked up by the OPP. After what I thought was a hot necking session and three warning from her mother that I should go home; I left at 1:00 AM to walk home about a mile away. Usually nothing would happen on this walk home (it may have happened another time) but this night this OPP constable stopped me and ask what I was doing and I told him "going home." He offered me a ride. I refused but he insisted. As he took me home he kept asking questions about this guy and that guy but all I could tell him was I knew them but that was all. Then he ask if I knew if this coming weekend there would be a fight some place for he had some dental problem and if he was in a good fight then the department would pay for the work. This brush with the law as innocent as it was disturbing and all because I was dating this girl. Starting to see how diabolical she was.

Broken heart! We dated for 3 years. I was loyal except for a few indiscretions when she was in Ottawa. I had to be careful as her older brother lived in Bonfield and he watched me like a hawk. She was a year ahead of

me in school so it was only in her second year at teachers college that I went to college myself in the Sault
Ste.-Marie. In my second year as this love or romance
(as the stomach turns) at what seemed to be the end
of the earth; she began to teach and in some ways we
had talked about marriage (quiet my wife just walked
by - ok she's gone) but I was still in school and I was
suppose she figured going out with a boy in college
wasn't as cool as one might think. When I came home
briefly that following summer I knew things were a
little odd when she suggested I quit college. She said
her brother could get me a job (shift work) and without
hesitation I said NO because all I had was one more
year to graduate. Turns out after she broke it off (she
broke my heart I swore of girls for a day) .To her I was
being unreasonable and selfish and every other lame
reason that I wouldn't leave college for her. I found out
she was going out with this high school wonder that
had a job and a car and they had been dating for some
time and eventually married. That was the real reason
to take my heart and walk all over and blame me for
it. Not to be kicked without getting up again I went to
the city and met up with a buddy. We went drinking
to ease the pain. I needed something so I dropped in
to Kreske's and there like an angel at the cash a raven
beauty (we can mention her, after all she did become my
bride). Denise I had hung around together in grade 12;
so I put on the charm and asked her out and she turned
me down. Now I had two excuses to get plastered. She
called later and said she changed her mind and would
go out with me (I had a policy especially when I was ½

in the bag to say "too bad, so sad", if you turn me down you do not exist, I will not be humiliated again or have my heart broken and so I said "maybe some other time".

Taking unnecessary risk! Outside of the fight on the hockey rink there were yet more stupid and unneces- sary risks yet to come (again caused by this temptress and as I think back her whipping boy and gofer). In the summer of 67 the economy was down the toilet and there was no work and as much as I tried there was nothing, especially living in this town the size of a stamp, I was going to college and didn't even have the $250.00 needed for tuition. I finally cornered this friend of my uncle Leo. This friend had a trucking business hauling pulp wood (4ft long logs) to paper mills. I volunteered my services (135 lbs on a good day) to load trucks for (ready) $25.00 dollars for a 6 day week (7 am to when we got home). I had a job and if I didn't spend any of it I would have tuition. Done deal! I probably wouldn't have lasted more than a day for this was physically hard work but dad said I wouldn't last a week and so early to work home for supper and straight to bed was the hallmark of my summer of 67. I got good at it and the boss let me take the truck Saturday afternoon to the lake for a wash (this is the unnecessary risk part) and drove it past her house even though I didn't have a drivers license. It seemed to be a worthwhile risk to take with this man's only way to make a living so I could impress this bimbo. God was truly present as nothing happened. I'm having so much fun blaming her for everything I did wrong!!

The inability to talk or speak or reason has to be given credit to all girls or women that I found attractive or cute, especially if they displayed dramatic feminine features such as beautiful eyes, perfect nose and long hair, a few other things but just can't remember off hand. Asking a girl to dance or going out I needed to muster all the courage I had with the driving force to get closer to these soft goddesses. I just wanted to touch but at the same time in every one of these girls the long arm of the law (mom) would say "sa s'appelle touche si pas) in other words look but don't touch till you are married or till I was 30 or she was dead whichever came first. You see being a good catholic to touch a girl outside of helping her get up or helping her with coat was punishable with a strait path to hell. So if I went to hell it's all because of those girls and women (LOL). But you see mama didn't raise no fool for I had an ace up my sleeve. There was always confession and I think they put a plaque in the confessional booth in Bonfield with my name on it. I digress. Too bad they didn't give frequent flyer miles. I could have gone to college by limo instead of the bus or thumbing it.

Even though all these she-devil's tried to take me away from mom (they didn't know what kind of force they were dealing with) she still managed to get me to pick berries for her and the family every day during raspberry and strawberry season. As I now reflect that I was so preoccupied by the ladies that I didn't realize or clue in that Roger was not included in our berry picking adventures (he never made picker of the month but I did). Maybe it's because I always brought home a full basket or more (mommy's boy curses) and Roger's basket was as empty as the one he picked up in the morning because he ate everything he picked and he would have eaten mine (if I didn't have the holy water with me he would have) LOL. I always kicked myself in the morning as I saw that infamous basket on the kitchen table (I can hear it now pick me, pick me) with the words from mom "get ready aunt Therese or Simone will pick you up real soon" gasped and ready I was to face another day of black flies and bears and hoping I would fill my basket early. For you see, these were not one or two hour trips. They went from sunrise to sunset (picking bees much like quilting bees) the women I picked berries with were possessed by the berry-demon and you did not play around for this was life or death and I pity the bear who would come near our berry patch.

I had many summer jobs all of them paying less than the poverty wage, from loading pulp trucks to 3 weeks on the CPR section gang and shoveling dirt into pickup trucks, cutting the cemetery lawn and looking after the grounds of the local convent. The one job I would like to forget is the one in 1964 where I went from an innocent country boy to a scared boy of the real world. Uncle Antoine, with good intention, got me a job with the extra gang (railroad) that he was in charge of. It was my first job away from home and mom wasn't too pleased to see her angelic boy go away and work with such folk (she was right). The job was that of cookie that is the cook's whipping boy. I had the pleasure of pealing a fifty pound bag of potatoes and what seemed endless carrots every evening before bed. I didn't have time to do it during the day between setting table for

30 hungry ill tempered men who were intent on finding every little anomaly and gripe about it. Between meals I got to the dishes next to the coal stove (a good thing I was skinny otherwise I would have charred my cute little bleep) it had to be on even though it was 80 deg. F. (+30 Celsius) outside as we needed the hot water which sat on the stove. All of this was included in the holiday package and was paid $200.00 a month with free room and board. With this all inclusive vacation came with cooks or chefs of every form and oddities. One was a French cook who made the best rice pudding ever but he busted my chops at everything little thing I did wrong. Another was a drunk who basically let me do the cooking shouting instructions from his bed (I never knew that if you drink too much you can only lift your drinking arm and nothing else). Anyway I learn to cook and clean all for the low low price of $200.00 a month. Then came the child molester who tried to get funny with me. But before I could get to my uncle and tell him the S.O.B. took off and for two weeks I was the chef and cookie for real as there was nobody else again for the low price of $200.00 a month. There are other interesting characters on this luxury cruise were alcoholics of every age, an old circus (20year old maybe) bump and a few ex-cons and a few family men like my uncle. They were all part of a family of misfits (a United Nations of people unseen and forgotten by society) that worked hard all day. The social outcast, if you will, would spend pay day on Dominion street (Borgia street.) in Sudbury on booze and women. This all took place between Lively and Cartier and I remember because on the day I got

hired on in Sudbury I was told to go out to Lively and meet up with the gang there. So off I went hitchhiking. But none of you would pick me up so I walk all the way from Sudbury to Lively (I hope you are feel sorry for me and bad about not picking me up). I went from 16 years old to a confused young man who had seen too much in too short a time. It was good to be home in my own bed where berry picking seemed pretty good.

Earlier on I spoke about working for the local Sisters of The Sacred Heart who by far, were the best nuns that ever kicked the habit. They were good to me as I cut the grass and lifted heavy objects you know the whole nine yards. They were always very positive and willing to go the extra mile. As for example in when the 11 and 12 grades were closed I was entering grade 12 Sister Carmen offered to come down from Ottawa once a month so that I could take geography by correspondence. It wasn't offered in the new school chosen by my parents (another story). Even in college we kept in touch. She was a great lady and cute as a button. This is where I found out they do have hair under their veils (walked in on an older nun as she was going from one room to another as I walked in to do something) I have never seen a nun run so fast (flying nun). I didn't know what to say or do, close my eyes or laugh. Anyway, she lived and I was more prudent the next time I went in the convent. I had this same sister (Sister Carmen) in grade 10 and I remember that I would stop and get a bag of gummy bears on the way to school after lunch and hide them in my desk. As the day went on I would secretly take one out when I thought the sister wasn't watching. The thing was I never tricked her. She knew! When I would go out for recess she would treat the girls to the candy. Eventually she told me and lesson learned. She was a great teacher.

Now the Sisters I encountered in North Bay were a whole different kettle of fish. I was used to the sweet sisters of Bonfield and now I found myself in an infested mine field of "you might have done it that way where you came from but not in my classroom" or "take your attitude out of this classroom" or "who do you think you are anyway?" So I stood up for myself and that got me in more trouble. Either I looked the wrong way or smiled at a pretty girl and oh yea, missed a few assignments. Boy! You make one little mistake and they throw the book at you. You guessed it. The Sisters never really accepted me or had warm fuzzy feelings for me. But that was fine I didn't care for them and I didn't want to go to school there. But mom and dad said well this is where you are going to school, case closed. I suppose it might have been my attitude but I like to think it was because I wasn't one of their trained rats they had since grade 9. Kids that had moms and dads who had the money to support this separate school. In my case, I paid for it myself from the money I made working during the summer at the paper mill my father worked at. They controlled most of the kids from the concentration camps of grade 9 to 11 and forgave the rich kids and the rest they hung out to dry. My dueling partner was Sister St Raymond (mother superior) and from the first chemistry class we hit it off with a bang. She asked a question and then asks me to answer it. I knew the answer but she called me Raymond and I stood up and I looked at her and said "my name is not Raymond. Either you call me Mr. Raymond or Patrick". It seems teachers or nuns don't like to be corrected in front of all the class (who knew). Well, that was a home run. Next was my homeroom teacher Sister St Simone who from what I heard she had been in the convent forever and seemingly nice enough but one day she started to humiliate one of the students (the student deserved reprimand) but extra homework not the really nasty comments. You could tell that for some reason she had enough and boom she went off on this tangent. So I stood up and challenged her attitude and told her this was not a Christian way of treating others and walked out. You think I was the most pompous (maybe) ass in the world and questioned if I should remain at the school (all my friends were at another school so why not me). My mother fixed everything and apologized for my behavior and said that it wouldn't happen again. Well I wasn't having any of it. So the first opportunity I got I went after Sister Grenade who was the choir director and would come into our class once a week for guidance class to help us find our way in the outside world. Any way this time she came as usual and didn't teach. She just got the girls from the choir and started choir practice. You can see where this was going. Yes,I got up and demanded she teach the class. After all I was paying out of my own pocket here and the one getting up at five in the morning to come to school because the government wouldn't pay for transportation for separate school children and I wanted my money's worth. She

called me a country hick from Bonfield like she was
any better. She was from an even smaller town in the
same back woods. I survived that brush with death (not
at school at home mom was livid) managed to keep a
low profile after that and I think the Sisters knew it was
better to let the sleeping dog lie. One thing that made
going to school worthwhile was that in our class they
put two desk together making more room available. I
didn't care because they put me right next to this really
cute blond (Joanne it's okay my wife likes her) and so we
had a school dance and since the never to be mentioned
girl friend was in Ottawa I asked Joanne if she would
be my date and she said yes. The Sisters found out about
our secret romance (one date) and on Monday morning
I found Joanne's desk moved all the away to the other
side of the room and someone else was sitting next to
me. I lost it and challenged them on why only the two
desks were changed and they said they had rearranged
all the desks. I questioned them on what are the odds
that by change all the other desk ended up in the same
place and these two didn't. This was their way of making
me pay for not buckling under. They took away the only
reason I would go to school, that and the long legged
raven beauty in grade 11 (another story).

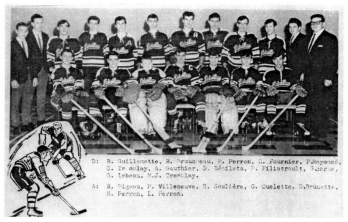

D: R. Guillemette, R. Brousseau, M. Perron, R. Fournier, P.Raymond,
C. Tremblay, A. Gauthier, D. Décileta, P. Filiatrault, G.Barbe,
G. Lebeau, M.J. Tremblay.
A: R. Pigeau, P. Villeneuve, G. Soulière, G. Ouelette, D.Brunette,
R. Perron, L. Perron.

Hockey team grade 12 top row third from the left

I slept on this ranting of the sisters and I took out some of the comments to be fair to them. They tried to be good teachers and some were. Others were bitter and maybe in another time they would have done something else, but committed as they were to their vows they tried to mold us into real people. When I wrote about them I think I was 18 again and finally allowed myself to express how I felt. This is something I was not allowed to do. Nobody ask why this good boy became such an ass. It didn't matter if I was happy or that what I wanted was that important. Everybody made decisions for me and now at 18 going on 19 I was probably saying "enough I don't care what you want, please just listen to me". I guess I still wanted to be that little boy with Mr. Roy who answered all my questions and made me feel so important. Now all I had were people telling me what to ask and then not to bother answering my questions and demanding I fall in line. God bless you Sisters! You, without knowing, saw the end results of all that bitterness and anger. The worst part in all this is the rest of the kids thought I was all that and more for standing up to them. It stroked my ego but trust me I didn't need an audience. I needed someone to see me and acknowledge me as I was with the Chinese man, the old fellow at the arena and Mr. Roy. Was it so hard for them to stop and say o.k. Pat, what do you want, we hear you and we see you. Oh what I wouldn't give to be that little boy again, playing ball with the big kids.

The year ended on a sour note when I, without bragging, should have gotten the award as best athlete (cross country champion, third in the mile in the NOSSA tournament, hockey) but they said my marks weren't good enough so they gave it to the son of a wealthy woman the head of the PTA. Well to be honest I did fail English and really never graduated (49 in English) Sister Raymond of course was the English teacher, honest to a fault and not one percentage point of mercy. Well I went to college anyway (yet to come). See the pattern here again? A woman or girl crushed my dreams. Not all my dreams! As the year unfolded there were some positive experiences. This is where I got to meet that long legged raven beauty Denise my bride to be as we hung around together. 6 or 8 of us always seem to be together, just friends and fun to be with. I wasn't interested in anything else but a plutonic relationship and if you believe that I got some swamp land in Florida or a bridge in California that I could sell you. LoL

Before going any further I would like to share my summer of 1966 when I had the honor to work at the paper mill in Temiskaming Quebec for the summer. The whole concept was that we would stand by the phone 24 - 7 and if they needed someone because someone didn't show up for work they would call us (my brother and me). The only thing wrong with that we stayed with dad +7 miles away and to get to work we had to walk. Normally that took around a 1 hour and ½ at least so it meant we got a 6 hr shift instead of 8 hrs. Every now and again we would know ahead of time like shifts on Tuesday was almost a sure thing as it was clean up day. That meant we would get these short shovels so we could get to those areas under the peelers (they took the bark off the logs) after sitting there for a while all wet and stinky, we got the job to clean up (now understood why dad said this is nothing when we had to shovel manure for the garden). This and getting to clean the ash out of the furnace which by humane standards was inhumane but people left you alone. This was a whole shift sweating and ash flying all over including under your clothes and itch like nothing I can compare it to as well as a shade cooler than the Sun. Nobody had to ask where you worked that day as only the lips and around your eyes were white. Then came the stacking of logs to build up those piles of wood you see in pictures with the nicely piled logs all around. These logs would be all ready peeled. When wet they were as slick as snot but with a wood pick and good luck you were ask to keep piling these logs around and to allow more logs to be piled on for future chipping (me at 135 lbs and logs from 30 to 50 lbs) on solid ground yes but on marbles dangerous and scary (I think this is where I got gifted with hemorrhoid).

Next there was the blow pit where they cooked wood, then drained it from the huge pots (cooked with sulphuric acid) and the sulphur stench would kill a skunk on a bad day. As pulp came out from the cooking pots and we had to use these power hoses, they were chained because of the power of the water and the entire wild allowed us to direct the pulp on. But the sulphur smell gagged you even with the gas masks and then you had snot coming out of your nose nonstop you might just get an idea how wondrous these shifts were. The only great thing was lunch. After being in this hell whole and now as you bit into your sandwich and discover everything tasted like sulphur. Dad worked there long enough and being the cook (cooked the wood to pulp) he didn't even wear a mask and had a good laugh watching his boys experience enough of his world that they would never think of not going to college. It worked. I swore that nothing would ever get me in one of these mills again. I got one souvenir from all this and that was that both my hands were burnt by the steam near the rollers as the paper came out to be rolled into large rolls for shipment. You see when the line (paper) broke we had to run under these large steam rollers and break the paper so the guys could grab a good end and restart the process. This time I must have got my hands too close and the steam burnt both insides of my hands. Big blisters! Of course they were not jumping for joy that a summer student had an injury. Then the rest of the 3 weeks I had left, they gave me jobs pushing buttons and graveyards watching conveyor belts. The last shift, I left, walked to the highway and thumbed my way home. The summer was mostly a bust as most of the time was spent waiting by the phone and I wasn't going to walk 7 miles into town for fun because I would have to walk back and maybe miss a call. Oh what joy! I hated that summer and to boot I had to pay for my own schooling (high school) and as Roger was now at college and he had a car and if he needed money guess who would dish out what he needed (how could I say no to mom). I really didn't feel warm fuzzy thoughts about my older brother then. The relationship took a turn for the worst when I wrote to him as he was now working and me in college and asked him to send me some money. He wrote back that I should be smarter with my money. This resentment for Roger eventually went away and today I love him as I said earlier. Then the kick in the pants or around there is that the following summer there were no jobs at the mill or anywhere else and that's why I took that job loading pulp trucks to pay for my tuition and live on a student loan $800.00 (room and board $80/ month X 8 plus books and clothing, and so entertainment and my social life at college was none existent) and I hitchhiked home for the holidays because I had no money for the bus. This was not a happy time for me as life was sh_____at best. My teen years died in a pile of disappointments and an ashen gray view of what was to come .I felt lost and almost hopeless as I watched all others around me with cars, money, girl friends, hope and nice clothes and popularity and all I could do was go to school, go home to a small room to someone who couldn't boil water. She took our money and fed us Klick and more Klick. Sandwiches with thick cheap margarine and Klick found themselves in my lunch. Every day! It tasted like sewer residue and then came supper fried Klick and frozen vegetables that tasted like paper. Oh the anguish. To top it all you were not allowed to go in the fridge after supper. Yes you're right. I just jumped into my college years and it was not a good start. From this lady who was in this for the money to a long line of women and girls that would make my college years frustrating (socially, physical, heartbreaking and so ever frustrating). I think mom sent a letter warning all good girls should stay away from her boy and all the other girls would pay dearly if they were even in the same room as her son. Mom put a curse on my love life. That's enough about the super powers of my mother.

College picture 20 yrs old

I'm getting ahead of myself. Let's start from the beginning the very first day and that is getting to the Sault.
Mom found out uncle Leo was going to the Sault
therefore he would take me (a trip to the Sault in those
days was like going to the moon. We never left Bonfield
) but for uncle Leo just another adventure. Uncle Leo
was the uncle who would leave with a half decent car
and come home with a beat up pickup truck with two or

three cages of live chickens as he made this deal with an old buddy. So as talented as he was mechanically he just couldn't turn down a deal. Anyway off we went in this beat up old car that he fixed once or twice before we got to the Sault. The house where I was to stay seemed nice enough at first. It was like buying that used car from this greasy hair dude. You know the one who promised that if anything goes wrong just bring it back only to find that he moved out of town during the night. The lady was nice enough when I met her and her husband (just think of that evil women from 101 Dalmatians and you'll have a good idea of what she was like after). The only good part of this was that there were other guys living there as well. They introduced me to the school which was about a mile away. No big deal. Walking was part of life back then (I guess today's kids can't imagine walking anywhere after the age of 10).

Frosh week came and went and I settled into a routin of getting up, going to school and coming back home. I didn't fit in. Most of my classmates were men that had made career changes and went to the bars after class. I was under age (the vow I made at confirmation) but mostly because I was under age and had no money and was a geek and so I lived a very uneventful first year of College. I learned how to stay awake and cram for exams for if you fail the final no matter how good your year was you failed and this was not an option. I guess this patch in my life reads as boring. Well, you have no idea how boring it was for me. The only reason I went to college and took Geology is because the Sisters told me I wasn't smart enough to go to University. Since I like Geography they suggested I take Geology (word to the wise they may both start with geo but they are no way anything alike) but it's not because I had any choice. As I was told, you start something you finish it. And.so I stayed.

Then the summer job came around. The first job in geology field exploration was with Newmont Mining. The main reason they chose me was not so much on my grades but because I was bilingual. You will see this will come in handy as the summer unfolds. First I met the man I was to work with. He was a renowned prospector or should I say his father was a renowned prospector who discovered what ended being Jerome mine. The son of the man was from Wanapitei. We did some prospecting right around where he lived for 2 to 3 weeks because where we were going there was still ice left on the lakes. This was not good for the planes. So I witness the dark moonlike borders of the Sudbury basin and found this kind of work as boring as watching paint dry. Soon enough we were off to Montreal by plane (you didn't think we walked did you?) No, this is not where my French gifts came into use as we went from one plane to another as to land in Chibougamou Quebec. No this not where I needed my French. You see my prospecting buddy knew two words in French "deux autres (two more)" and as long as he could get the first beer he was good as he would order deux autres and everything was hunky dory. Eventually we took a Beaver (plane) canoe and enough stuff (tents, food, and every little thing anyone would need to survive) but no gun. After all we wouldn't want to shoot a bear who was just grocery shopping noooooooooooo.

Anyway for about a month (ah yes some of the lakes still had ice on them as we are 200 miles south of James Bay).This prospector and I would do a preliminary survey of the glacial debris that would kick the Geiger counter and so we spent the summer trying to follow the glacial debris back to its original source (needle in the hay stack would have been easier). But this meant that about every 10 days or so tearing down camp moving and setting up again (one time as I was tearing down and picked up my cot up I found a nest of garter snakes. From then on, trust me, I knew what was on the ground before I set up my cot.) But when we set up on a new site it was always near a lake and the boss liked to fish (native land shhhhh) so we would go fishing always keeping an eye out for the forest ranger flying over. I have never caught so many fish in my life from speckle trout to fresh water herring, pike the size of (well one time I needed to make a noose out of the anchor rope to bring in this one pike that was too big for the net or my hand and it was at least 4 to 5 feet long. I got a picture here somewhere). This last pike still had the lure my partner had lost the day before (this fish got away from him yesterday). It was all catch and release and the occasional meal. The fishing made the summer go by faster as there was a mail strike and all we could get on the radio was Moscow and the Inuit channel. Trust me, things got so bad that we stop talking to each other (this is where the French came in so handy). He was mad at me because I had twice as much reading material than him and I kept explaining that it wasn't my fault that the can of soup or other cans had both English and French. Now I know why we were not allowed guns. LOL

Then the prospector left and they sent this accomplished Toronto geology student to work the next two months with (the only rock he ever saw before this was the rocks on Toronto buildings). I am sorry but we were fresh out of buildings and he had no bush experience what so ever but he was in charge. All this for $375.00 per month and all the black flies I could eat. Think about all these black flies hungry and nothing to eat and here come meals on wheels fresh from the south. The flies were so bad when it was time to go to the bathroom you sat with cheeks in the winds and a can of Raid spraying between your legs. We did find the remains of a bush plane from years gone by. I can't remember if the crash was ever found before. It was an eye opener as we flew in these same planes every week. Hardly saw any wildlife. There was the occasional moose and a herd of caribou but not much of anything else. It was lonely so we would eat and work and sleep; we had to be careful with the meat and eat the pork first (kept meat under the moss near the permafrost but I remember this one time we thought that the pork chops might have a short shelf life so we decided to cook and eat them all (21 pork chops) and then laid down on our cots with pop, cigarettes, chocolate bars and chips and moaned. I put on 25 to 30 lbs that summer. Like the bears, I had to fatten up for another school year. This one time we camped on this island and it was infested with mice. Everywhere you looked or stepped there was a mouse, so we opened a trap line to see how many we could catch (did you know mice love peanut butter). Every morning we would check our trap line to see how many we caught. That's how bad it was getting. One day I did get scared as this Torontonian decided we should head for this huge outcrop (big black outcrop) in the distance and off we went. The thing about this part of the world is that there is nothing but swamp and tag alders and so walking in the bush was always a chore at best. One thing we needed to remember was that about 4 or 5 o'clock every day it would rain. Anyway we went and got there around 11 am, looked at this outcrop and now it's time to go back. Now we need to follow our compass to get back. That was no problem as I had done it before. So off we went, him leading and for some reason we were going in a circle. After 4 hours we found ourselves still back at the outcrop. Now it's raining, getting dark and I asked him if he had made the correction on his compass for magnetic north and true north change as you go further north especially this far. He said yes now I'm getting scared and p___ off and demand to see his compass. Sure enough he hadn't made the changes. I guess he thought we could just look for a street sign. Fortunately, I had made the corrections and I suggested that he follow me and by the grace of God and the advice of the old prospector who told me "always adjust your compass" we got home (camp) as it was getting dark. We were cold and wet to the bone and hungry and again saw the wisdom of no guns allowed. He got up the next day and suggested we go back out and in a few words, suggested something else. There was some tension from then on and he was a little less pompous.

So soon enough the end came on a rainy summer day as I called in on the radio to announce to the world I am back , AND THE PILOT SAID TO CALL BACK ON THE RADIO WHEN IT STOPPED RAINING. I watched the rain for 72 hours and as soon as that last drop of rain fell I was on that radio. Out we flew right into Chibougamou airport for the flight to Montreal (note to those who have never spent any time in the bush you need to remember to keep the flies away you do not wash clothes or 85% of your body as to survive the endless buffet spread before all these black flies. As we entered Montreal airport (I developed a Moses complex) it was like the parting of the Red Sea as people just got out of my way. It was suggested that I take a shower (they had a place you could do that). A shower helped but trust me sandblasting would have been better. Anyway, from there I took a bus to North Bay. I remember sitting on the bus and someone asked why I was wearing such a big knife and that's when I realized I was no longer in the bush (free at last). When I got home mom ceremoniously burnt my clothes and made me take at least 2 to 3 baths. I know I make light of this experience but as I reflect on those days, everything we did every day mattered as we depended on each other as there was no one else to lend a helping hand. I remember once when the pilot picked us up to move again we asked him if he smelt smoke and he added yes there's a forest fire not 10 miles from here and said "up here we just let them burn themselves out". I thought to myself what if the wind shifted would we be part of just let it burn itself out. About three days home and off to school I went. I was different and so was my relationships with you know who; something was off.

Second year wasn't going to be much better if not worst but I assure you that I got to know a lot more girls (not in biblical way) as they knew if they had a problem with their SOB boyfriend they could talk to Pat. It's amazing how many times the girls would say "Oh I wish I would have met you first" and I would say to myself "I'm here now". Man that p____ me off! I was good enough to console them but not good enough to love (I was still going out with you know who) but a boy has needs and this plutonic relationship crap was just that, then finding out she was cheating on me and I couldn't get anyone to cheat with really added salt to the wound. Now that's pretty sad. I went home for thanksgiving and that's when this new working teacher lowered the boom on me almost demanding I quit school and go to work. I got the impression she (a teacher) couldn't be going out with a student with 2 years of school left. As we know, that was the end of a less than perfect relationship. I had a broken heart. Well you know the story. So I went back to school. Not long after I called mom about leaving, and going to the Trappist monks. Mom suggested that I should finish what I started. This from mom was a surprise as she always wanted me to become a priest (not a monk)

Moved around from one apartment to the next and finally ended up with a class mate that took me for a ride. That was another experience. I needed money to eat so every Friday night we held a poker night for students under age who wanted to drink and play poker. I would wait till they got drunk and then I would play sober (never could get the hang of drinking) and clean up making enough money to eat for another week. They wanted to drink more than anything else so they kept coming back. I got back on that dating circuit and with a bang I started dating three redheads at one time (dangerous at any time) but being close to financial ruin I had to drop two of them (it's rough when the economy bottoms out). I wasn't cheating I was just being nice to girls that happened to like me. Peggy was a cute little Irish girl (her father drank and often found it unsettling as this was the complete opposite from the father I knew) I could tell she wanted to get close but every time things seemed good she would back off and couldn't see herself trusting a man just yet. We had some good times together. I thought that we could make it work but she couldn't get past the trust issue. So we became friends and like I needed another friend, she would be my connection during the summer as to finding an apartment for my third year. Before the summer rolled around I got a letter from that long legged raven beauty Denise and this letter changed my whole life and my outlook on life and gave me a purpose I never had before. We wrote to each other and we agreed to meet during my spring break. So I found myself hitchhiking on this beautiful spring day with 25 cents in my pocket. A spring jacket and a bag with clean underwear and I got a ride that took me to Elliot Lake turn off and as fate would have it as I got out of the car it started to snow (wet heavy and lots of it). I went in the gas bar and got a cup of coffee (costs 25 all the money I had). I got back on the highway and eventually a nice gentleman offered me a ride. Wet and cold I accepted. He asked if I would help him get out of the ditch if by chance we slid of the road. Sure enough twice. But a ride was a ride as he was only going to Sturgeon Falls because I was such a help he drove me to North Bay. I'm telling you what a man won't do for a woman is unbelievable. Hitched from there to Bonfield, had something to eat, cleaned up and said hi to mom and hitched a ride back to North Bay, got to Denise's house, knocked at the door and her father answered with "which one are you". A little set back,I introduced myself and he said well "she's at school". So off I went about 3 or 4 miles walking (that's what you do when you have no money) to meet her at school. That's when my forest fire for her started and has been burning nonstop since (like the pilot said "up here we just let it burn"). The smoke detector just went off. LOL. We wrote back and forth and it started to get serious not like in the movies jumping in bed kind of serious. How we felt for each other became something special and something we could call ours (remember the curses of mom "don't touch" and for that I thank you mom).

The fire was lit but we knew better than to play with fire. As the summer came I got a summer job in Red Lake (not the town the bush working for Shield Geophysics). This was somewhat different and that is the reason why they hired me was to shadow this new geologist from Poland (it was the time when Poland was trying to break away from the USSR) who spoke

better French than English and I was to help him with
English geological terms and rock types etc. He turned
out to be a really nice guy but only stayed for a while.
It was a large camp, three tents plus eating tent with a
French cook. Man could he cook! I gained weight even
though we worked hard. It was nothing to eat two or
three T-bone steaks for supper with vegetables and pie
and on and on. Every meal was like you never had a
meal in days. This was only to last for a month or so
then I was sent to a secondary camp which had an old
Hudson Bay cabin long abandoned. I was to bring all
the gear for geological survey by canoe. This canoe was
so overloaded that a straw added would have sunk me.
Off I went, hugging the shoreline and praying the wind
wouldn't pick up. Otherwise, well things ended well. We
found ourselves in a pretty nice set up. We were 4 com-
bined with 2 linemen (to run survey) and another cursed
Toronto geologist (student who had one good arm) and
you guessed it I was to babysit this idiot. The problem
was that in this area when you went into the forest you
never touch ground as you were always walking on dead
falls (must of been a huge wind at one time and pushed
over endless trees that lay over the floor of the bush)so
you literary had to jump from one tree fall to another.
This was hard enough with two good arms so I would
spend my days picking up this geologist as he would
eventually fall between the dead falls and couldn't get
back up and what made it worse he would bitch and
complained about everything. It got so bad that we
would draw straws to see who would babysit today.

Again, this was a good reason why there were no guns allowed in camp.

Everything worked out as they found out I was a pretty decent cook so they agreed I should stay in camp, keep the place clean and cook. There was a time when I suffered from a bad abscess. It was so bad I couldn't even eat spaghetti, couldn't sleep and again it rained for two days so the planes couldn't come and get me. It near drove me out my mind the pain was so bad. You may chose to believe this next part or not but it is the truth. We had problems with a bear who kept coming and doing his shopping at our food storage. We tried everything but he or she was persistent. So in my insane mood I set out to challenge said bear. I figured since we had a porch on this old cabin I would hang a slab of bacon in the doorway and wait by the door. I had heard that if you hit a bear with the blunt end of the axe you could knock it out so I stood by the door waiting for said bear and you know if you use the blunt end of the axe it can knock out a bear long enough to kill it (me 1 Bear 0). Kids, don't try this at home.

After all was said and done I tried to get back in the cabin but the guys had locked the door. God was present. Got out and spend a week in Red Lake (you haven't lived till you stayed in Red Lake) and got the tooth pulled out.

This is where I bought Denise's engagement ring. I saw it in this small jewelry store and when I saw it I knew that was the ring and it was. I was getting $450.00 per month and I was just storing it away. But again that curse was to rear its ugly head as Denise in her letters pleaded with me to come to her grade 13 prom. I finally agreed to come down and ask the boss for a week off and he gave it to me. So I took a bus from Red Lake to North Bay; now that's a midway ride for you. So now I'm this stud muffin who will show my gal a good time. I rented a car for the prom and wouldn't you know it a block from her house this guy rear-ended me and not knowing what to do or how these things work out. I trusted him when he told me "don't call the cops it's not that bad. There's not much here so here is my number and when you get the estimate call and I will pay". You guessed it. The next day I brought the car back to the rental and the estimate was $800.00 and of course the phone number was bogus. This drained my bank account and I had to borrow money from Denise to get back to Red Lake. Here I was, only two months left to make enough money to finish school. I ended up with enough for 6 months with the student loan after tuition and books.

Third year was eventful as it being the year I talked a friend of mind to come back to school. Told him I would help him until he got back on his feet as he applied for a student loan. We got an apartment together and my choice of friends never ceases to amaze me and of course, he like my brother, had a car which was great except for the fact that I was paying for everything. Any money he had went into the car (snow tires etc.). We survived on a dozen wild ducks he had frozen with bannock on the side (lard and flour fried in a frying pan). He loved his liquor. He got lucky the first week there and she was over all the time (they were doing the dirty deed in the bed next to me 3ft away small bedroom). Life was just peachy three years and nothing and him in only 2 days. Eventually the money ran out and we were asked to leave. He swore he would pay me back and I'm still waiting. We were lucky that my best friend Butch had great parents who took us in. Lodged and fed us for two months. All I knew is that I wanted out and as far away from school as possible.

Denise did come up once and mom found out and gave her a letter to give me. Being mom, she told me that I should be careful, that it was worth waiting and so on. Little did mom know that I had made arrangements with one of those girls that cried on my shoulder? They had a place for Denise to sleep while she was here. After three years and a lot of confusion and a lot of drinking, fragmented relationships, struggling to be independent, letting go of my youth, my innocence, Iwas looking ahead to a new chapter and at the same time holding on to what little of the past I thought I needed. I went from school, to work. I didn't even go to my own graduation and this time I did graduate (put that in your pipe and smoke it Sister St. Raymond). Here I was 130 lbs soaking wet, long hair, no car, and ready to face the world (yea right). Here I was. It was like I had a pilot's license, had never flown a plane and was expected to soar on my own.

Adulthood!!!!!!!!!!!!!!!

I MANAGED TO GET A LOAN FROM A FINANCE COMPANY, as the bank wouldn't touch me to buy a used car for $800.00 (Chevy Biscaine), It was maroon with 4 tires and a steering wheel and brakes, 4 door sedan. It was like a dream. Two days at home and off to Sudbury to build my future and start paying for this car (not one day working and I had payments on a car and student loans) I had arrived. I was an adult ready to face the world. I got into Inco and with a quick interview of upper management in our department I was told that I would be going to Levack mine. I asked for an advance so I could get gas for my car and they more or less told me if I didn't have money for gas what was I doing with a car. Anyway they gave me the advance and arranged for me to stay at the bunk houses in Levack and that my room and board would be taken out of my pay check that plus the advance made. This made the first few checks on the light side ($550.00/month) take home was $80.00 per week after I paid for the advance. Then I threw in payments for a wedding ring as we decided to get married in August. That gave me three months, almost 4 months to build a nest egg, pay for the wedding and find a place in Sudbury and I tell you finding a place in those days was like finding a unicorn. We finally got a place in a Chelmsford basement apartment for $150.00 a month. But it wouldn't be ready till the end of September. Fortunately someone from the mine had a cottage on Windy Lake and was renting it out. This became our first home and honeymoon all wrapped up as pretty as you please. During the summer I connected with my uncle Jacques the second youngest of my mother's siblings and as it happened he being a teacher, was going to his cottage for the summer and asked if I would watch the place for him.I agreed and moved out of the bunkhouses and was able to save on the room and board.

Uncle Jack

Little did I know that uncle Jack would become probably the only true friend I would have. Even to this day. He died 25 years ago, not a day goes by that I don't miss him. He was all those men I met as a boy. He took time to listen and cared about what I thought, was nonjudgmental. He embraced me as a brother and played a major role in my life that caries me even to this day. Few men could ever replace uncle Jacques. As I watched him go through the death of my aunt Delorese and as he himself fell to cancer at a young age. We would visit, laugh, cry and pray together. We shared very personal struggles. We shared in our struggles in how to raise our children. He was a scholar, a teacher, a man of wisdom, a loving father, and patient to a fault, an uncle, golfing buddy, and my best friend. The greatest gift he ever gave me was that I was one of the first people to whom he announced the devastating news of his cancer. Thank you for allowing me into your life and feeling that by telling me, about your illness, that I was also important to you. God is present. I miss you Uncle Jack. I wish you were here to talk to, to hold me, to carry me, even to go play a round of golf (haven't play much since) but most of all just to be my friend.

Wedding picture Aug. 29, 1970

Denise and I never wanted any fuss made over our wedding. A wedding at the church with a meal after with family would have been perfect. The wedding itself was beautiful up to the part that father Brunk who referred to me as this lug said to Denise "Do you promise to obey?" (she said yes) and also I remember that the wedding march was The Russian Anthem. I remember being very nervous and how beautiful Denise was (I finally did something right). But mom wouldn't have just a simple wedding since this was her first child to get married. It was going to be done right. So decided they would pay for the meal. We decided to invite family and friends and Denise looked after most of the preparation such as music (juke box) allowing people to play their favorite songs (Roger the best man thought it was funny to play and replay (Lay Lady lay). When we went home to change we anxiously went through the cards and collected the money and got enough to pay for the hall (nothing like living on the edge). So we were able to enjoy the rest of the evening. After the reception we headed off to a small hotel not far from my parent's home. The only trouble was Denise was hungry and wanted to go to my parent's house for they were hosting family and friends and since nothing was open (I knew if we did go there be no end to it). She settled on the gift mom gave her which was two small potatoes with a small carrot held together with a toothpick. Denise laughed and ate the whole thing. The rest of the evening was delightful and mom was right about waiting.

The next day we dropped in to see mom and dad for breakfast and off we went as far as 10 miles short of Sturgeon Falls where I had rented a small cottage so that we could rest!!! After the long hour drive from Bonfield. The next day we got to Windy lake and settled in as it was the long weekend (three days to get married not bad). The next day I went to work and ran out of gas in the parking lot. Luckily it was pay day and I walked to the bank and I got some cash (I didn't have a penny to my name),bought a can of gas and fueled up so I could get back to Denise. That month on the lake was out of this world but it had to end (the apartment was ready). For the apartment we got a card table and chairs from mom and dad, no TV (made up on own entertainment) a fridge I bought for a $100.00 (kept for over 30 years). Uncle Jack gave us an old stove. Only two elements worked and a stove that had a mind of its own. The bed was my grandmother's old metal frame and the mattress sagged in the middle (perfect). We were happy and Denise announced that she really didn't want to work, she wanted children. I think she got pregnant before the pills hit the bottom of the trash can. God is present. We had a wonderful year. We laughed (Denise has a laugh that warmed the coldest part of any person),we walked in the rain, we took our clothes on a toboggan to the Laundromat. I put the car on blocks for the winter. We didn't have much. I sold most of my camping gear to buy Christmas gifts. We were so happy. We waited patiently for our first child (Denise was never sexier). The great day arrived when Tyna (Boots) was born. She was a strong healthy baby, as cute as a button. I was a proud father and Denise was a glowing mother. This was truly one of the happiest days of our lives. In less than a month our world was turned upside down.

Denise lost the use of her left hand and side as well as the sight in the left eye. She would walk on her behind so as not to drop the baby. She would put her hand between the diaper and the baby (cloth diapers) and she knew the pin was through the cloth when she saw blood on her finger. For me I didn't know if I was coming or going; I lived in a haze. I had lost my bride, the woman I loved to M.S. This word continues to haunt me even to this day. I was married to Denise for one year and now I had to learn to love another person (yes inside she was the same but we don't live on the inside). With time she was able to regain her ability to function somewhat normally and we learned to get through life as two different people. I had changed as well as she had. Her ailment affects not only the person but also those who love and lived with her. I often say to myself I Married Denise three times, once in 1970, 1971 and 2015 (to be visited later) and would do so again if need be. What has changed is not the love but how to love and for that I thank God.

Life was difficult financially, emotionally, and spiritually. We now went to the English parish because the first X-Mass I was at the French church and asked what time Christmas Eve Mass was and the gentlemen told me that I had to pay a dollar to reserve a seat for the mass. Well need I say more? I quickly told him that I wasn't interested in paying for a seat in the church and found the small English parish St-Alexander's who welcomed us with open arms and became a fortress of strength for both of us. The whole thing didn't start of that great as I asked Father C. if we could talk and explain to him that Denise had M.S. and that I needed help spiritually. The first thing he told me was that he had M.S. I remember telling myself "who cares what you have I'm here about me". He was a blessing in our struggles as he understood the disease and became a very close friend. He was the first to ask if I would be interested in the deacon's program. I was but life was too busy and I wasn't ready to take on more. We went to see a specialist. Those first comment sent me into a tail spin. He said "I want you to know that M.S. is not caused by venereal disease". You can image how I was ready to kick his ass as I was here to get advice and all I get is this ignorant S.O.B. who was more concerned with bullshit than medicine. I never felt so alone and lost. I just wanted to scream and I knew then and there that even if I screamed nobody would hear me.

Denise started playing the organ at church and I started reading at Mass and life seemed to have balance. With bills and trying to buy a house, we approached the adoption agency concerning adoption. They turned us down because they thought that Denise had sclerosis of the liver (drinking disease). Again our cries for help were unheard. We found ourselves asking Father Clark if it would be okay to take a risk on the M.S. and have another baby (they had told us that the first major attack was caused by the delivery of our first child). He sent us to see a specialist who told us that it was not true. He also told us that we could have another child. The only thing was that if Denise did have an attack it meant we would now have two children to look after. Well he hadn't finish saying, Denise was pregnant for our second daughter Renee Claude (Spark). So we had a 4 year old and a new little girl and all was well. Denise always told me that the best she ever felt is when she was pregnant. It seems that the body rejected the M.S. while she was with child. Yes I know all we had to do is keep Denise pregnant and everything would be fine. Things should be so simple.

We bought our first house. It was a townhouse and thanks to MPP rep, who helped us save our home as the contractor was a crook and we nearly lost everything. But by the grace of God we didn't. I began coaching minor hockey and getting involved with the running of minor hockey locally and in the Sudbury area. Why didn't Denise leave me is beyond understanding as I was putting in 40hrs a week at work and 40hrs at the arena and that left little time for family. I would drag Tyna (she wouldn't let me leave unless I took her along) to my practices and games. She became the water girl and all the boys looked after her . That left Denise at home with the baby. As I look back she must have felt lonely at times and never said anything. I was a bit of an ass. We lived a pretty normal life, made friends and life was good. We had our problems and never really had an all and out fight. We tried everything from freezer plan to powdered milk to try and save money. Amazingly, Denise never complained and I would like to thank her for that.

I have to give Denise the shield of honor as my fear of snakes became crippling. One day as I drove into the driveway I spotted a snake right by the car so I beep the horn until my spouse came out to kill it so I could get out of the car. You know who wore the pants in the family. We continued to be active in our parish and even took a marriage encounter weekend which was great. We tried many things to try and build up our relationship as a couple. I had more growing up to do but Denise was patient.

Renee was born in 1976 on Valentine's Day. It was one of joy of course and yet the saddest as Denise's father passed away 2 weeks after Renee was born. God is present as for Mr. Ranger never did leave North Bay. But as my mother in law was coming to help for a few weeks he decided to come and visit for one day. This meant everything to Denise and they sang together (he was choir director and he got to see our new little girl). Two weeks later he died from a heart attack. The following November my father died from a brain tumor. Roger and I got to see papa in Toronto when we heard he was to have the surgery. I never saw my father weak. He was always strong, like a big old oak tree. He died 2 days after the surgery. They gave him maybe 2 yrs but jaundice set in and took him. He was 57 too young. Now mom was alone with 2 young girls at home. It was a rough X-Mass and New Year for this was dad's favorite time of the year.

Getting older started to suck, big time. I never understood why my mom was crying when her father passed away. I remember asking her why she was crying (I was about 3 or 4) and she told me that her father had died (I do remember being at grandma's and the body was in the living room). It was only now at 28 did I finally understand mom's tears and her pain. They say bad things happen in threes and sure enough Uncle Jack's wife Aunt Delorese died in February the following year, almost a year to the day. We had had enough of death and found ourselves back to a normal existence as Denise's health and ability to get around was good. Mom went through a few rough years. We all tried to help her as much as possible and like Denise's mom; she was very resilient (always saw her as a strong woman). In 1978-79 mom met a man with the same family background as dad - Robert never married and I'll never forget her asking my permission to get remarried and of course I told her "If this is what you want why not". They got married but my two youngest sisters still at home didn't care for him, especially Claudette, dad's pet never accepted him as part of the family. She always said that nobody could take dad's place. This made it hard for mom but Robert gave mom financial security and someone to talk to (More to be said later). So when the offer to go to Thunder Bay came up at Inco I accepted since mom was better off and I thought this would be a good career move. Denise and I were apart for 2 months as the selling of the house and relocating would take place. Inco looked after everything including plane fair back home every couple of weeks. This was the first time we were apart since we were married and it felt odd at best. We finally got everybody up to Thunder Bay. It was different for us and the kids. We were now 15 hour drive away from our families. We had no friends or church community to help us in times of difficulty. The great gift of this move was that in 1980, Dawn (magoo or papoon) was born. We celebrated our tenth anniversary 3 days later in North Bay - yes we were down for my sister's wedding (Rose). Dawn could always say she was born in the Bay not Thunder Bay but North Bay, we rushed to the hospital. Denise wanted to stop at MacDonald's to p---- . Good thing we didn't as this little girl would have been born with large red shoes and a red nose. Dawn was on express delivery and we just made the hospital. I promised not to mention that Denise's water broke on the way all over the front seat of our new Catalina. Red velvet seats and all we had were wet ones (note to self always carry large cleaning rags and cleaning agents in the car). There I was at midnight in the hospital parking lot, in the dark, trying to clean this not so pleasant (that's putting it mildly) odor. I could not clean my seats and its over 30 degrees outside - brought it out to the car dealers the next day and they steam cleaned it but I swear I could still smell it on hot days until the day I sold it. That was a nice car. Who cared? My third daughter was born and then and there I knew I was a rich man. As the preacher would say praise the Lord.

Before I go on, I would like to speak about our three girls:

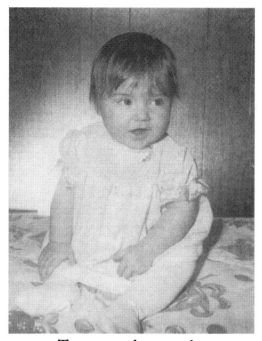

Tyna around 12 months

Tyna was our first daughter, we called her "Boots". When she was in the crib, we were so afraid to cut her nails as she was scratching herself. I needed to figure out a way to protect her. They didn't make mitts for babies at the time. We had a lot of booties people gave as gifts with some of the most useless get ups. So, I put boots on her hands and it worked. From then on she would be known as Boots. She was the most beautiful baby ever and I have pictures to prove it. She was bright and curious. I remember one time when we lived in this rat hole of an apartment. The floor had a big enough slope that Tyna was able to go to one end of the apartment with her walker and lift her feet and roll all the way to the other side.

I had grown a beard and one day, I decided to shave it off. She watched me do it. As I washed up, she screamed and took advantage of the slope and took off. She was very special to my father. She was their first grandchild. He would sit her on his foot or knee and sing a song that sounded like" didalee didalee" so she started calling him grandpapa didalee (she clung to him like glue and you could tell that suited him fine) .

Puzzles, fruit, no candy, polite, she was the perfect child. We thought we were the perfect parents. She willingly sat on the potty for hours (it seemed) at a time. She would sit in front of the TV with snacks. Denise would tell everyone she was potty trained (I think she probably still has a permanent ring around her behind).

We discovered that she had a lazy eye and surgery would be needed and she had to start school with a patch over her left eye and you know how cruel kids can be. She never complained but you could tell it wasn't easy. But, she got through it. She followed me like she did with Dad. She came to every hockey practice and game. We gave her a jersey and a hockey helmet (this helmet would come back to haunt our second child Renée). They were good days. The players treated her like their little sister. We gave her a trophy: Trainer Tyna.

I just remembered Tyna wanting to play tee ball. I can remember that every time she came up to bat she had to go to the bathroom (she would be up there squirming like a fish out of water). God bless Tyna. No matter the sport outside of swimming an athlete maybe not so much. A musician much like her mom.

Up to grade 8 things were seemingly okay as now we found ourselves in Thunder Bay. We had moved up there when she was 10. She excelled at school. The one thing I told all my children was that lying wouldn't be tolerated and Tyna couldn't tell a lie to save her soul. She had a canopy bed and we painted a mural in her room back in Chelmsford (drawn by my sister Rose and cousin Murielle). She so loved that room with her black and white 10" TV and boom box. When it came to going to high school she made me eat my words: "you can do anything you want if you want it bad enough and are willing to work for it``

She was and is a very accomplished flautist and piano player and suggested that she could go to high school in Ottawa since there wasn`t a French high school in Thunder Bay. The government would pay for the school of her choosing. Off we went for an audition and she got in. I did everything in my power to prevent it but found out very quickly I was not in charge. It was a hard year. With her body changing, living with a strange family, she did well at school but when I told her we were moving back to Sudbury and there was a school (Sudbury Secondary) with a music program she jumped at the chance and of course the school and we were happy to have her around.

Things were different now as she became distant and unpredictable, ready to challenge me at every turn. I experienced a true artistic temperament with the extreme highs and extreme lows. As I look back there, were times I was too hard on her and vice versa – she was willing to talk to me at times. She told me what was bothering her and then she would shut me out. I paced the floor on many nights worrying about her – feeling helpless and so afraid of losing her as she was trying to discover herself. Even to this day she refuses to take criticism. Her whole persona changes even when I try to help. I suppose it`s probably more that she wants me to see her as able and don't need dad`s help. It will always be a struggle between me trying to help and her trying to break away.

Many hours spend outside the Judo class and music lessons, skating lessons, swimming lessons, dancing lessons and happy to do it. University was another kettle of fish, as she needed to go to Western in London Ontario, probably the most elite and expensive she could have picked. Laurentian didn't seem good enough. Unfortunately things didn't work out so of I went to London to pick her up there and back in one day. She got a part time job as we awaited her new start at Laurentian. I got her a car which was cheaper than Western or any other out of town University. This is where the sparks and struggles came to life. She wanted her independence. I was trying to hold on seeing the pitfalls and traps she was to experience.

We would have down and out verbal battles, but I refused to let go and she was determined to break away (not one of us was ready and I guess we never are until we do cut the cord and hopefully both could tread water). Tyna became a teacher and got married had two boys (Patrick and Max) unfortunately like her mother she was shackled with M.S. This affected her teaching career and her marriage. One thing about Tyna, she is a person who refuses to give up and ready to prove others wrong to a fault when it comes to her abilities.

Her gift is her ability to work with children and relate to people. A gift she got from her mother. She is most definitely the image of her mom in all ways. She loves her music, communication, and love of children. She even looks a lot like mom and they both have M.S. I think in some ways she sees herself in Denise. Being on her own, she is uncertain about the future. Not to say that I am that special but I am here for her mother and there is no one there for her. I will worry about this girl all my life – I am the first man to love her. I don't take that lightly and I need to believe that God is ever present for he loved her before she was in the womb. Tyna will always be the one I seek out when I need something done when it comes to mom and also seek her advice on how to proceed.

Renée Claude 18 months

Next is the child that bears the name of Denise's deceased brother Claude. Renée Claude, was better known as "Spark". The first time I saw her she had this impish grin on her face and I said this is trouble in the making. Being a Valentine baby, all that came to mind was the Valentine's massacre. Wouldn't you know it she like me, likes gangster movies, so I wasn't far off. She would always be the one that trouble would find on a regular bases. A good example was the time were we were at Uncle Jack's cottage. She decided to go swimming. Just for a moment, I looked the other way and when I looked back Renée was drowning. She was going down for the third time by the time I got to her and pulled her out of the water.

Renée was always the curious one, and like Tyna a good baby. Sleeping was not a problem through the night. She was always very social, true to her nickname to this day. She wanted to dance, be a model (as active as she was, she was probably the most girly girl we had). I may get shot over some of the things I say here but this is how I see these things.

When we left for Thunder Bay, Renée spoke no English and within a year there she refused to speak French. There was only one French school and we were determined she would learn French. Her refusal to speak French, we decided put in the English system which set her back a year. But this is what made her happy.

She once told all the kids in her class that she was having a birthday party. This one Saturday came and people were coming to our door for the party. The problem was that it was nowhere near her birthday. This is the kind of stuff she would pull off. Once in Thunder Bay, being the girly girl of the three, she decided she needed nail polish. Since mom never used any makeup, she thought that the liquid paper I had at my desk would be just fine. So there she was as proud as a peacock prancing around with her white nail polish.

She is the one who would put her younger sister in a sleeping bag and push her down the stairs (telling her this would be a great slide). She was the one who escaped through the bedroom window because she was grounded. I found her near the church waiting for mom to come out of church. She loved to go shopping. She followed me on most of my shopping trips.

I'll never forget the time when I got her a bike at the police auction. It was, as she would tell you snot green (it was). But what broke the camel's back was that I made her wear the hockey helmet her sister wore for hockey (to this day she still talks about the kids making fun of her but all I can do now is smile). We eventually painted the bike black and that seemed to help but the helmet stayed.

She was not one for the yard and liked to wander. School was not a priority, but playing pranks on others seemed to be a calling. Once she called the people from the hair replacement ad (TV infomercial). She used my name with my info. From then on, I kept getting all this info and propaganda on hair replacement treatments and the spray can etc. She even had Depends send a sample to her younger sister. She thought she was so funny and as I look back, she was.

She was, and continues to be the one with spark and a laugh that is contagious and brings energy to our family. That is truly her trade mark. I wish she would have put as much into school work. But that's water under the bridge. She didn't finish high school. What with a premature stork activity, that changed her life. She made some mistakes that affected her life and still does in some way. She married and had a second child Ailla sister to Skyler.

Unfortunately the marriage was abusive and she found herself moving back home with two kids and all her furniture. I have to tell you, it was crowded but it was better than being in this abusive marriage.

She remarried with Richard and now they find themselves in Corunna (near Sarnia) with two more children (Anna-Kate and Noah). She has been successful in opening her own Hair Salon and with her husband working at one of the plants in chemical valley. They find themselves comfortable. The thing you need to remember about Renée is that as a child she inhaled life, every waking moment was worth living to the max.

She found great joy in locking mom out of the house until mom uttered those words of doom "I will tell your father". She couldn't understand why mom didn't find it funny because to her it was hilarious. Renée wanted her sister Dawn to be born on the road (trip from Thunder Bay to North Bay) and that I would have to deliver the baby. She thought that would be great (see what I am working with).

The only time she freaked out was when we saw E.T. in the mall. She didn't care for that at all. I couldn't believe this child, who dared everything became terrified of a mascot or stuffed animal. I guess E.T. or any cartoon character in costume was her kryptonite.

The cadets became for her a new feather in her hat. She did well in a disciplinary environment. She made it to summer camp. She left as an awkward teen and return to us, more grownup in many ways.

The violin was another one of those needed things that fell to the wayside. She thought that by simply picking up the violin she would be a protégée. After her one lesson dismay, she discarded the quest for stardom.

She was always protective of her younger sister as only she could push her sister around but no one else. She was the prototype mother bear with her cubs and that is especially true with her own children. She loved art class and hated every other class. School was in the way of her living her life. Even though she never finished high school she has done well for herself. Renée will always be that ray of sunshine and the one who is not afraid to act with in your face attitude.

Dawn 5 yrs old

Dawn (magoo or papooun) is our third child. I don't know why the name magoo but it seemed to rhyme. If you know the dynamics of this family you would know that all my life as a father, I always tried to keep a balance between the girls everyone had 4 gifts at Christmas. If one had a birthday I would make sure they all received a gift, and if one had a nickname they all should have one - like the two older ones.

She was a great baby. Dawn was the baby that I spoke about earlier. She was our tenth anniversary baby. As a baby, she was quiet and hardly a fuss. She was very affectionate, love to cuddle and also liked to follow me around. I was off on Fridays and her sisters were in school. I would take her everywhere. Never had a word or demand and always curious. I had to watch her as she would wander off. She had a big wheel, which she put on enough mileage on to go around the world. She could make that thing dance and she inherited the hockey helmet.

The one thing that drove her was seeing Tyna read. She had to learn to read and did so at an early age. Dawn and Tyna both read and inhaled books. As for Renée, like her dad books are good as door stoppers and sleeping pills. Dawn appreciated everything you did for her and wasn't one to demand or ask for things. She like school even though we were in Thunder Bay she went to the French school. As we moved back to Chelmsford she attended the French school to finish of her year (Kindergarten). She asked if she could go to English school with Renée. We didn't want to go through what her sister went through. The school did have French immersion.

She had the uncanny ability of slacking up until Christmas but enough to pass. So we would have the talk and she ended the year as the most improved student. She excelled at soccer and loved to play against the boys .She loved to dance and did well at it but those in charge kept bumping her up with older girls and wanted her to come in more and more. They managed to spoil the dancing that she loved and then quit.

We found out that she had a reading disorder (when you read some things and see them backward). They picked this up in high school but she managed to do well with the same rhythm as previous years graduated. Even though her guidance teacher told her she should look into making jewelry more or less telling her she wasn't college or university material.

In high school she excelled in Volley Ball and drama. She proved them all wrong she took social work at college and then went to university (put that in your pipe and smoke it). One thing about Dawn: never tell her she can't do something because she will prove you wrong. Dawn is a mixture of her two sisters: smart and has no problem tackling problems. I often go to her when I am at a lost and needing advice on how to proceed (she is an old soul reminds me a lot of mom).

She is a good mom always looking for ways to improve Sadie and Jack. We now have 8 grandchildren. I wanted 10 but kids never listen. As a teenager, she had a dark side that I really didn't find out about till later. She was always one to keep to herself emotionally. She would look to mom and her older sister for help while the other two came to dad. I always assumed that things were ok, but not so. Only through the grace of God, her sisters, and her mother we were able to get through it.

I got to know Dawn better after she got married and I found myself retired. I would get together at her house and I would bring her soup and yogurt for the kids as I was going to work at the funeral home. I miss those 20 min or 30 min quick lunches, they meant a lot to me as I got to know her more as a woman. I think in some ways I always saw her as that little girl (miss her also). The girl who had the worst luck: she stepped on a broken bottle in the park, got her finger jammed in the washroom at the Sault Ste. Marie bus stop.

Maybe funny that Renée always seemed to be around and got the blame for not looking after Dawn. The worst was when mom went to Barbados with grandma. Not one minute after she left, we hit the Oreo cookies only to have her bring them back up. Now I had taken holidays to stay with the kids, she was as sick as a dog. We both missed mom I guess for different reasons.

She, as well as her sisters is gifted. With her, it's pottery or working in clay sculpting. I am grateful that she took the time to learn quilting as this is in honor of her grandmother's claim to fame. Again the old soul comes through with knitting and looking back at art forms that allow her to express herself as an individual.

One thing that was peculiar to Dawn and that is her sleeping habits became more predominant when we moved back to Chelmsford. The house had three bed-rooms downstairs off the reck room. Little did we know that during the night she would often get up to watch infomercials as we slept up stairs? How we found out was at X-mass when the three put on a skit for us. She had memorized these infomercials to the letter; so if you need new hair, slicer dicer, or newest gadget just call Dawn at 1 800 555 1111 and if you call within the hour we will double this offer with no extra charge.

The one thing I liked to do was to take the girls out for lunch together or separately. I got to know them as women, mothers and wives. We are truly gifted with three girls that God trusted us to nurture and raise to womanhood.

I would like to tell everyone how proud I am of the three greatest gifts given to Denise and I. The grand children are the icing on the cake and yes I wanted 10. They have been great teachers to me. On how to be a father, they blessed me with council and opened my eyes to women issues and I have to admit they were often right. Probably the greatest gift they gave both Denise and I, is when they come back home and allow us to be part of their lives. We made a lot of mistakes and ask that they forgive us for those mistakes. It was always for their wellbeing as our primary goal. No man could love these girls as much as I do. I only hope they can love their own children as much.

Tyna 10 at back, Me and Denise, Renée 6, Dawn 2

Specks of the past with the dynamic trio:
One summer trip, we (me) decided to take a trip. It was to see their uncle Guy and Paul (Denise's brothers) in Toronto, with Tyna 7 and Renée 3. We took the train to Toronto and Guy took us around Niagara Falls, Toronto Zoo and Marine Land. Tyna being the only one to come She lost a tooth hoping to cash in with the city tooth fairy. She did get 5.00$. That with the dollar father Brunk sent to her when she was born. I owe her $6.00 just try and collect. We went back to pick up Renée in North Bay and then took off to Ottawa by train were Renée thought this was an opportunity for her to drive

dad crazy with her train exploration. We went to visit Paul another brother of Denise's. When we arrived, Paul's girls thought it would be great to give Renée a bath in there Barbie doll pool and they did.

We would often take the train from Thunder Bay to come down for Christmas. As much as that seemed like a good idea, the Renée express would travel from one car to the next getting to know everyone she met. She knew the stewards who would help her cross from one car to the other as there was ice between the cars and slippery. I never knew from one minute to the next were she was except at night when they had a bingo that she had to go.

The one thing about having girls is that before you got 2 ft out of the station they new and used every washroom within walking distance. Bus wasn't much better as they could sleep. Denise could sleep on a rock, so they would sleep and rest and I would be wide awake and as pleasant as a summer breeze.

By car, train, or bus it was never really a good experience especially the trip from hell. 17 hours from Thunder Bay as the car broke down in a small town. We had to wait for the garage to open as the mechanic didn't start till 10 AM and we had left at 5 or 6 AM so we had three kids up since before the sun rose and now with nothing to do and we running out of gimmicks to keep them happy. We still had another 9 hours of family time in the car to look forward to. You see, our families said it was too far for them to come and visit so I suppose it was shorter for us.

Renee, the charmer (instigator) sat between the other two and in her role as instigator kept the other two especially Tyna on their toes, it's a good thing I didn't keep my promises otherwise I would be writing this from my prison cell. On one of those trips I had made a faux floor with padding and they could sleep on it. With a small black and white TV that could catch the odd program on the trip. I was ahead of the times as well as ridiculously brain-dead when it came to safety. God was and is present.

One thing we did on Saturdays was tape music. I acquired all the music I could get together. The one I taped the most was the Jesus Christ Superstar soundtrack. Several times this had to be taped as my kids would wear them out. Especially Renée and Dawn, who knew every part by heart and could, sing any part on request. Dawn's favorite singing role was Pontius Pilate and Mary Magdalene. Several Saturdays were spent shopping as dad likes to shop and so did the girls.

The one thing I remember was this one small mall that had a kiosk with bulk candy and chocolate and we would always end up buying what we liked and something new to try (rosebuds with coconut for Denise).

As I reflect on life with Denise, I truly feel I was hard on her in the first few years. I think maybe I refused to accept the M.S. I threw all my energy into coaching hockey and umpiring little league baseball. I refused to grow up in many ways but Denise never said much she just waited for me to grow up. This didn't happen until we moved to Thunder Bay. We needed to depend on each other more and more. After she had a seizure, I found myself alone with two young girls and a 4 month old baby; I was scared. Mom or Uncle Jack weren't down the street. I had to man up and look after business.

Things changed and I found myself falling more in love with my bride. Some of the aside events were like teaching math to Renee using candy especially on subtractions as it turned out it would have been better to have used $$$$$ signs. As I look back, Denise was such a good wife and mother and put up with a lot of my neglect and selfishness.

Maybe I need to remember all those years, as now the tables are turned. We were always Sunday Catholics but not always good Christians in our life style. I now see how important a healthy spiritual environment is needed to remain strong in ones life. It`s amazing that in Thunder Bay, our social life was healthy but cost me anyway a less than a healthy spiritual life. We made lifelong friends that didn`t share our beliefs but were supportive and always looked after us as we were the younger couple.

One Christmas we (me) decided not to go home and spend it alone. Seeing how much we regretted my decision, friends invited us to Christmas supper with them (thank you Bill and Sharon). This is the year that mom sent me a cassette she expressed her sadness as we wouldn`t be there for family Christmas. It broke my heart to hear her open herself to me, how much these family meals were highlights in her life. We were so far away and missing so many. It saddened her that her little boy and his family would be absent. I never missed another meal especially Christmas.

After being 6 years in Thunder Bay I saw that I needed to get a second job. Inco had a shut down and left me with half my normal salary. The new job was a security guard (I was In better shape than now as I was a body builder in the gym 4 to 5 times a week). The job paid enough to make up the other half of my salary if I worked 6 shifts a week. I would get Tyna babysitting gigs for hotel guests. I remember one anniversary; I got a room with champagne and a new nightgown for Denise on the bed. I invited her to come and see where I worked and asked the front desk if I could show her a room (wink wink) and the rest stayed in that room.

We moved back to Chelmsford and life changed for the better and the storm of adolescence loomed. We seasoned parents forgot to board the windows and head to higher ground. Boy what a mistake as the eye of the storm got closer. We kept telling ourselves this will be over quickly. The first storm or hurricane was hurricane Tyna as the teen years were not friendly to me. We struggled in our relationship as she hit the coast of dating and choose the wrong boy. She had the power to cause tornadoes of "I am old enough that you should trust me" stripping the roof of her dad's trailer park of sanity. That mixed in with floods of misjudgment that washed away common sense and cause a waterfall of anger on my part. These were stormy days in our relationship.

Tyna married later with a man who thought he understood what it meant to be married. I tried to explain what it meant to be married to someone who has M.S. (education my ass). She left him after she had two wonderful boys and she got tired of having to take care of three boys. He never understood that in marriage, we at times need to give a lot more than the other person, even though both give 100%. We would have to give 150% because the sickness could demand more from us, as it took more from our spouses. He was more into taking than giving (I am a man take care of me). This is not the girl I raised as I always told or reminded my girls that they had value and that they mattered. It took a lot for her to leave when the future was so uncertain. Back home with furniture and two boys . Note to all who have children: the girls come back and the boys leave and I have proof. Tyna is a music teacher and gifted individual.

Before going on if you have girls, hope that they should be ugly as sin, like a caterpillar and at the age of 30 they go into a cocoon and come out like butterflies. It would be easier on everybody, especially dad. If not this, at least allow fathers to forget what being an 18 year old boy was like and not have the anxiety caused by old memories. I had a good memory unfortunately.

Renée Claude was more like a cold war as her dating was more behind enemy lines. I would have had to be a stealth bomber to get any info on her dating plans and relationships. Few boys came to the door and all seem to be innocent enough. That should have been my first clue. Unfortunately, I thought by having a less in your face attitude that didn't work with Tyna it would easier- but it wasn't. The stork was early, crossed enemy lines and we found ourselves to be grandparents.

A new dynamic evolved as now I had to make a peace treaty with the enemy as we needed to find an apartment. Skyler was the new member of the alliance. Things were difficult for them and we tried to help her as much as possible. Unfortunately, her furniture and broken heart landed back in her homeland until she got back on her feet. I still have some of her stuff (I have to get on that purging). All is well today as she finds herself with 4 children (Skyler, Ailla, Anna-Kate and Noah). They are all different and special in their own way. Her husband Richard stands by her side. Peace at last. She owns her own hair salon and is good at her craft.

Dawn was a curious balance. I knew she was going out with boys. Like her sisters said "dad got soft and she got away with murder". Unlike the elder sisters Dawn was never in your face. Maybe she was sneakier or smarter but was good at reassuring dad that every-thing was cool. Maybe I just wanted this to be true. Her dating was like being on the bus in Paris and having your pocket picked and not know what happen until it was much too late.

At this time I would like to thank Bell for the $20.00 long distance bundle as she was on the phone for hours with her future husband Devin who lived in British Columbia at the time. These phone calls would go on for hours. Dawn is married with Devin and has two great children Sadie and Jack. Dawn is a social worker by profession and an advocate for the marginalized. She, more than the others is not afraid to correct her dad on issues of today. Dawn will always be that little girl who loved her Big Wheel and a sense of adventure.

All of this wrapped up with schooling for the deaconate program. After talking to the girls and getting their opinion, we decided to dip our toe into the ministry program. The only concern was, as Renée put it: "as long as we don't have to go door to door" So off we went to a new page in our life. Father B. D. was the priest who guided me in applying- as I had thought about it but just put it aside. I would like to thank Father B. D. for his wisdom and gentle approach.

The other priest that had an impact was father M. B. who was there for most of the time, as we prepared and went to Espanola once a month for instruction. Father M.B. was very dynamic. Some saw him as a thorn and others as the rose. No one saw that with every rose there came thorns that can hurt. But there is a price we needed to embrace and accept such a treasure.

Father C M. was sent to us to bridge a fragmented parish into a new more stable parish for the next priest. This was Father C.'s call in the diocese. He went from one broken parish to the next. He would help mend or stabilize the community when a popular or other priest would leave. I really enjoyed him as he was no nonsense. He asked me once why I was doing what I was doing. He said that sitting in the pew would be the common sense thing to do. Why did I want to get into this side of the church when I didn't have to?

In my last year of discernment, Father R. was to become our pastor. A young priest, who wasn't afraid of allowing me to grow, and spread my wings, 1994 was the year I was accepted into the deaconate and Bishop Pappin presided. The funniest part of the ordination was when Father R. told me not to get nervous. He presented the auxiliary Bishop as the Bishop that broke the ice.

I need to talk about what happened before the ordination. Someone told me that all hell would break loose and that Satan would put stumbling blocks and try and stop the ordination. Well right he was. This is the time we found out Renée was with child (not married yet), Tyna announced that she had M.S.. My mother in law passed away 4 months before and my step dad passed away 2 weeks before the ordination. I remember Dawn asking when the ordination was as she was getting anxious. She was the only one left with nothing bad happened to.

Ordination and Mandation 1994
Pat Denise

Then came Father P.M., a close and dear friend who was just the priest I needed. I was in my first years. Father P. was a good companion in my formation as we shared the same sense of humor and continues to be my friend to this day. He would come over to watch our favorite sit-com and have supper every Thursday night before Mass. He also had the uncanny ability of getting things done by simply mentioning what was needed in earshot of those who could and would get things done.

Then along came Father S. who with all his dedication to the parish. He at the same time struggled with me. His strengths were his organizational skills and a strong connection with the children of the parish and school. He helped this parish move into a singular building after so many years of one parish in two buildings.

The one thing I appreciated in my time of transition was that the Bishop asked Denise if it was okay with her first. I always appreciated that. After 14 years at St. Alexander's I found myself going to St. Stanislaus, St. Pius X and St Christopher. I was also part time at the parish in Kilarney all with Father T. F.. The 6yrs with father T. were challenging and at the same time very educational. I learned a great deal about liturgy and felt more and more comfortable at the altar. Can`t say it wasn`t without turmoil and questions that challenged me when it came to where my loyalty should lie.

During this time I continued prison ministry at the Sudbury jail. It became a burden now. I was going to 3 – 4 masses on the weekend and then rushing to the jail for an hour and getting home at 3 on Sundays (had left home 6:30 - 7 am). I found myself dropping this ministry to focus more on bible study in the parishes that I had done for over 10 yrs prior to coming to St. Stanislaus. Then, we added a Sunday evening Mass, leaving me with no evening to have supper with my family and the grandchildren. Father had a way of making me feel guilty when I would miss the Sunday night Mass.

Denise was wonderful and still is with all that was thrown at me. She has always supported anything I did and do for the church. Ministry, as I came to find out, is a lot of work and sacrifice. With Denise`s prayer and help I can deal with it all. She is my strength and my prayer life. She is never critical of my dedication, and the only person that I know that see`s in me what I desperately look for every day.

The three years spent in Espanola in ministry program, was probably the most exciting and fulfilling years. Once a month we would have to go up on Friday and back on Sunday for 2 days of education , classes and preparation for the deaconate. This was after 2 years of scripture that I totally enjoyed. Every weekend would end with an assignment to reflect and write up and hand in the next ministry weekend I found this the most exciting as I was discovering more and more about the church, about ministry, about my faith and throw in a little psychology

Always amazed me the most was how I came to discover whatever new revelation I tripped over. I still have awe moments but fewer and fewer as the years go on. I've lost the zest. Nothing is asked of me and life gets in the way. But every now and again, I happen to read or hear something that rekindles that flame of new knowledge and new perspective.

The one thing I do remember about those three years was that the girls really didn't want to come for the weekend. My mom would come up and spend the weekend with the girls (I remember the girls reflecting on their grandma as she never stopped cleaning even to sweeping the outside walk and telling the girls that this made her happy). The girls were older now and requested that they didn't need a sitter. They would look after things but boy was I buffaloed. Everything, from broken windows, parties and God only knows what else.

We got through it – told them they needed to go church. On Sunday, they would send Dawn the baby to church and get a bulletin to give the impression that they had gone to church. This worked fine until I asked how Father B.'s homily was and they praised his homily. I knew he was away that weekend (one for dad 99 for the girls).

At ministry, people were always amazed how little time Denise and I would spend together. We would find our own place and that wasn't always together. We never felt a need to cling on to each other as we are two different people and that too should be celebrated. I think it was that we didn't need to be together 24-7 to know we were together.

In some way we looked forward to the weekend as it was an escape and a place we would gather with friends in this new journey. We were always anxious to share the enlightenment we experienced on our own. The prayer life and celebrations shared were shots of spiritual adrenalin needed. In as much as it was exhilarating as it was challenging when mixed with work and family life.

For 10 months per year it was almost like being in another world. Reflection, prayer, and sharing, I would seek out any one who would listen. This was also a time when I was involved with RCIA. Every opportunity was accelerated as we met with the candidates. In some ways I really miss those days of rich enlightenment and spiritual highs. Even as I write about those days, I feel that energy. God was so generous in his giving back then, and maybe even more today. It is still possible. All I need to do is be open and aware when those moments are given as grace.

In some ways I think it happens when I prepare my homilies and when I share those homilies. I am given another infusion of grace and new awareness. God is present. Before, I would share with one or two people.

God has blessed me with three communities who accept what God has given me and that in its self is evidence of God for me. When I started 22 years ago doing homiletic it was like standing in front of a shooting squad. The nerves were almost overwhelming. Trusting in God got me through them and as the years went on it got easier but never easy. For years it was once a month or even seven weeks depending on the priest. When father Pat came into my world that is when my homilies became more frequent. Words given to share are not words to read. One lady always told me she didn't need to hear another reading three was enough and that reading a homily did nothing for her.

Denise and I near retirement

Probably the most difficult and yet richest years were to come as Denise and I retired. 2010 I retired from Inco doing what I loved. Unfortunately, one small man who became my supervisor only wanted me out as I could retire at anytime and was not affected by his scare tactics. He threatened to put me back into the mines even though my knees were finished and I am now 62. I found myself at the H.R. and retired within weeks. This man was petty and willing to step on whom ever to promote himself. He was probably one of two bosses I had in 40 years that would sacrifice their own mother to get ahead.

Retirement offered new opportunities as Lougheed's funeral homes offered me a job as greeter and to do

prayers and then performing funerals. I was gifted with
the responsibility of 79 funerals in 2015. I did so many
funerals I thought maybe people would see me as the
Deacon of Doom. I always felt uncomfortable working
funerals as they are always awkward in what you say or
do as the person before you is in distress, hurt and lost.
I truly believe God always chooses ministries in which
you need to depend on him and in that way God can
work through you. All your garbage is just that garbage.
And as funerals, I think we need to feel all those things I
am speaking about because it brings to life the reality of
our own death and mortality.

God has been generous in giving me the ability to
pick up on the emotions and feelings people are going
through at the time of the service. In the homily, I
always try to make them feel that even though I never
met the deceased I found or discovered the essence of
who she/he was. The one thing I ask God for is to do
the funeral where my words are of value to the family
or friends. A lot of the funerals I do are estranged
Catholics and street people or people alone in the world.
If nothing else I try to bring validation or dignity and
respect to the individual who has died.

I've been avoiding this part of my story because it is
very personal and probably the one that is most hurtful
and yet most life giving. The life Denise and I share
is not something we verbalize or open to the world.
As much as a lot of people have had glimpses of our
struggle and even the love story we live. I want everyone
to know that we do have moments not worth mentioning, moments where I am less than pleasant, moments

were Denise is a diva. But through all of that, ours is a marriage that has glue and string holding it together and two people discovering themselves even today after 46 years.

Over the years we have shared and struggled with everything from finances and sickness, to the joy in the birth of our girls. I know I am just postponing the reality of M.S. in our lives. It has been a factor in how many children to have. If not for the M.S., I think we would have had 12 children, all girls. So it is a constant presence. Do we do this or that, even do we go for a walk or not. I don't want pity or "oh poor you" I just want you to know it's a factor in how we live our lives.

We always tried to live our lives without allowing M.S. to be a controlling factor but we always needed to be aware of the limiting factors. I always found it to be frustrating, being healthy and active and not always accepting what we had as compared to what could be. For 44 years we had some limits because of this unwelcomed guest in our marriage.

Denise refused to limit herself and always pushed the envelope. But on February of 2015, the ugly face of this unwanted guest reared its head and took away Denise's ability to walk. Never have I felt so useless and lost and found myself walking in a haze. After all, we knew this day would come but why now. We were just starting to enjoy our retirement and life was good.

Now I need to have people help me take care of my spouse whom I promised to look after. To admit that I can't is really a punch to the gut. To find I can no longing be her man, that I can no longer protect her. I can't be the husband that she married.

With all those reflections bouncing around in my mind, I found the common ground in all this is that it had all become about me. As much as it was Denise that couldn't walk, I was the one that needed the handicap sticker. The M.S. had not only taken over Denise but it had crippled me along with her. To say there aren't days that I don't feel sorry for me would be lies. Denise is blessed with a strong faith and refuses to be crippled spiritually or emotionally by the disease.

This allows me to move forward. I'm sorry I didn't go for those walks she ask me to go with her. I'm sorry about a lot of things I missed in years gone by. But I refuse to let the wondrous moments ahead go by without acknowledging them. We have the grand children and our three girls that care for us in their own way. Then the people from the parishes that hold us up when we need it. Elaine, Albert, Diona and so many more who truly care for our well being and pray for Denise and I. I had to let go of many things in my life such as work and some of my ministry. But I discovered that caring for my spouse is a true ministry. Life has been difficult at times. But most of all one of great adventures, moments of fear and awe, tattered rags mended together by the grace of God. Oh, what a quilt.

There are moments in my life I purposely left out as some are dark and I see no reason to validate them as they are scars I carry. I refuse to let a few scars stain the quilt God has patiently put together. I leave those dark moments in the hands of God, because I know for a fact that is where God was most present in my life. I have intentionally chose to speak about the positive moments in my life because that is what feeds the soul. Yes even M. S. can be a positive force if you place it in the hands of God.

God Is Present In The Quilt

I WOULD LIKE THIS FINAL REFLECTION TO ANCHOR this life story. Thank You.

I pray to God every day that he blesses those I love. But most of all I pray that he blesses every child in the world with hope. That they have someone they can turn to who makes them feel important and heard. No child should be without memories that can carry them through hard times. May every child have a Mr. Roy, a Chinese laundry man or even a stranger with a gentle hand and a giving heart? Too many children know war and pain as a way of life. Let us bring peace, and healing to these children so they can have a life. Their memories could be the face of God in the world, a world who so desperately needs Him.

CPSIA information can be obtained
at www.ICGtesting.com
Printed in the USA
LVOW12s0100131216
516996LV00002B/2/P